Further learning from the patient

Patrick Casement's first book, *On Learning from the Patient*, is a best-seller in its field and has been published in twelve languages. In this new, follow-up volume, the author looks further into the techniques of analysis and psychotherapy and focuses on what happens in the analytic space between analyst and patient.

Using many clinical examples, Patrick Casement shows the value of monitoring clinical work from the patient's point of view as well as the therapist's. This process of 'internal supervision' can teach the therapist new things, such as the patient's unconscious search for what is needed for emotional health and recovery. Stressing the importance in the therapist taking notice of the communication implicit in behaviour, Casement argues that the unconscious is a potentially positive force which can work constructively with the therapist.

Casement's development of original concepts, and his use of examples to deepen and clarify clinical understanding of the processes involved in analysis and psychotherapy, make *Further Learning from the Patient* of special value. It will be required reading for trainee and practising analysts and therapists, and for people who work in the caring professions.

'Few analysts convey better than Casement the actual feeling of work in the consulting room. His non-dogmatic but rigorous attention to the total communication of the patient represents what is best and most convincing about modern psychoanalysis. His book will be of particular value to trainees in the psychodynamic professions, but will also be refreshing to more experienced practitioners.'

David Black, Westminster Pastoral
Foundation in *The British Journal
of Psychiatry*

Further learning from the patient
the patient
The analytic space and process

Patrick Casement

ROUTLEDGE

London

First published 1990
by Routledge
11 New Fetter Lane, London EC4P 4EE

Routledge is an imprint of the Taylor & Francis Group

Reprinted 1991, 1993; 1997 and 1999

© 1990 Patrick Casement

Typeset in Times by Columns of Reading
Printed and bound in Great Britain by
Biddles Ltd, www.Biddles.co.uk

British Library Cataloguing in Publication Data
A catalogue record for this book is available from the British Library.

ISBN 0–415–05425–7 (hbk)
ISBN 0–415–05426–5 (pbk)

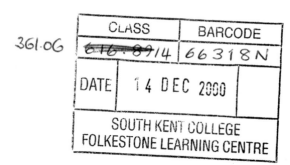

For Margaret, Hanna, and Bella

Contents

Acknowledgements

I wish to thank the many people who prompted me to go on writing, including the editors of various journals for their invitations to contribute those papers that formed the original nucleus for this second volume; also Harry (H.A. Williams) for his inspiration and encouragement to look beyond dogma; Fran Acheson, Dilys Daws, Martin James, Michael Parsons and Eric Rayner for help with particular chapters; Jim Gomersall and Gill Hinshelwood for their reading of the full text; and once again Josephine Klein for her painstaking work of editing each chapter, and the book as a whole, before it was presented for publication. Most particularly, I wish to thank 'Joy' (Chapter 3) for being herself, her parents for their permission to publish my work with her, and all my patients and students for their contributions to my understanding of the analytic process, without which I could not have written this book.

The author and publishers wish also to acknowledge permissions received to use material that has been published before, the details of which are given in relation to the chapters in question. I would also like to thank Faber and Faber Ltd for permission to reproduce material from *Four Quartets* by T.S. Eliot in Chapter 2, and from *Collected Poems* by Edwin Muir in Chapter 10.

Introduction

The psycho-analyst needs to be able to question
himself as often as, and as long as, he is un-satisfied, but
should not spend too much time looking for the answer in
books. The time we have is limited, so we must read people.
(Bion 1975: 17)

This is the second of two volumes on the theme of learning from
patients. In the 1985 volume I focused on the interactional
processes in the analytic relationship in order to illustrate the
patient's unconscious contributions to the analytic work, and to
show that theory is not just applied in clinical work – it is also
rediscovered. In this volume I continue to explore that earlier
theme, and also to highlight some further issues that are related
to the analytic process.

The emphasis in this book is again on technique, looking into
the rationale behind what analysts and therapists do. In particular
I look at issues of technique from the patient's point of view, and
I suggest that the benefits from using this viewpoint can be far-
reaching. For instance, it can help the analyst to recognize more
easily when some interpretations have ceased to be effective with
a particular patient because they have become too familiar.
Instead, when working more specifically with the individual
patient insight can be arrived at freshly (see Chapter 2).

Two themes in particular emerge from the clinical work
described here: the importance of analytic space (that makes
analytic understanding possible) and the analytic process. With
the help of these two reference points the analyst or therapist can
be guided towards working more effectively, monitoring the
analytic space for what may be intruding upon it and the analytic
process for what could disturb it. I return to these themes for
more specific consideration in Chapters 9 and 10.

1

When we follow the analytic process with an open mind (not burdened by preconception) it becomes easier to see how this process points towards what is being looked for – for recovery and for health. And what is needed often turns out to be quite different from anything that theory alone might have anticipated or common sense have imagined (Chapter 5). It then becomes clear how different is the process of analysis from Alexander's notion of the corrective emotional experience (Chapter 6).

The surfacing of insight often happens quite surprisingly. So does the re-emergence of unconscious conflict and past experiences still needing to be worked through. Frequently these come about in ways that may also represent key aspects of early trauma and/or environmental failure (Chapters 4 and 5).

The first patient I ever worked with already showed in striking ways how her unconscious search for the help she needed was expressed in symptomatic behaviour. That patient happened to be a child (Chapter 3). I have since come to wonder about the dynamics of this unconscious search for what is needed, which again raises the issue of meeting a patient's needs (or not) in analysis and analytic psychotherapy (Chapter 6). This eventually prompted me to suggest the notion of unconscious hope (Chapter 7).

An examination of the interrelationship between inner and outer reality further highlights the issue of 'environmental provision', whether in childhood or in the consulting-room, so that analysts should allow for the effects that they are having upon the analytic process – for good or for ill (Chapter 8). This again emphasizes the need for self-monitoring, so I suggest a number of ways in which internal supervision can be developed – to help in following the analytic interaction and in recognizing the implications for the patient of the analyst's ways of working (Chapter 9). This then leads me back to the sub-title of the book 'The analytic space and process' (Chapter 10).

As a link with the previous volume I offer an outline of the influences that lie behind the writing of both books and some of the ideas which form the basis from which I begin this volume (Chapter 1).

I cite authors whenever I quote from them, but I know that I am not able to designate all influences upon me: the thinking of others has often been a part of my own for so long that I cannot always recall exactly what I have learned from whom. Sometimes, however, there may be parallels of which I could have no knowledge because I had not yet read what many others have written. My apologies, therefore, to those authors who may feel that their works should have been cited. But I believe that parallel 'discovery' has its own value; and I think that clinical work feels specially validated when a path that others have travelled before is happened upon independently. The difference is that the analyst (or therapist) has sometimes been led to this by unconscious processes in the patient – not by dogma. Of course, we might arrive at the same point more directly by following the 'maps' that others could have provided, but insight that is applied too readily from established understanding is seldom as effective as that which is arrived at from working with the patient.

This book has been written with the same readership in mind as that of the previous volume. It is hoped that it will be of value to psychoanalysts and analytic psychotherapists – whether they are (like most of us) still learning or teaching as well. It is also offered to those many others who work in the helping professions or who are interested in the dynamics of human interaction. I refer interchangeably to 'analysts' and 'therapists' throughout, not because I think that the work of analysis and analytic psychotherapy is necessarily the same but to avoid needless repetition and because the interest in those dynamics that they have in common is the subject of this book.

Note: I continue to be concerned with the question of confidentiality and the ethical issues that arise from the use of clinical material from patients' therapy, and from students in supervision. I have discussed these matters quite fully elsewhere (Casement 1985: *Appendix II*).

Chapter one

Beyond dogma[1]

Because of the interest shown in my earlier book On Learning from the Patient *(1985), I was asked by the editorial board of the* British Journal of Psychotherapy *to outline the process of writing it and where the ideas came from. Prompted by that invitation, I describe here the principal influences that lie behind that first volume (and this) and some of the ideas that form the basis from which I am starting here, before I proceed further into the mysteries, challenges, and discoveries that are inherent in the analytic encounter.*

The search for meaning

Quite early in my life I had noticed two apparently contra-dictory forces operating within me. On the one hand I felt that I had to question everything – particularly anything that was presented to me as a dogmatic 'given'; on the other hand I was looking for certainty. In those days I thought of security in terms of being sure – knowing rather than not-knowing.

For a while I tried belonging to a group of fundamentalist Christians. They actively fostered a belief that they could offer the certainty I was then looking for; and, by contrast, all error and doubt could be relegated to others. (In those days I did not know about projection.) I therefore planned to read theology with a view to becoming a priest.

However, in my first year at university I studied anthropology. This helped to open my eyes to the incredible diversity of life; and I began to discover the 'otherness' of others – far beyond my previous imaginings. I also began to realize that, in any attempt to understand other societies – and people different from ourselves – we have to approach that task without preconception. If too much weight is given to what is already known, then the unknown remains elusive and our attempts at understanding introduce their own distortions to what is being studied. I thus came to realize that 'received truth' obstructs the study of what is new and different: a balance has to be found between what is already known and what is yet to be discovered.

When, after that, I still proceeded to read theology it was from a very altered viewpoint. I was once again challenging everything; but, this time, I was prepared to stay with my own doubts. I became a questioning agnostic.

Dogma and schism

In the course of studying theology I also read a lot of church history. Here another theme came to my notice, the paradox that human truth is never one-sided – nor can it ever be fully defined.

In my very first publication, an article entitled 'The paradox of unity', I wrote:

> Man's mind recoils from paradox, and tries to find some escape from this tension either in a form of absolutism or in compromise. . . . Much of our present theological disunity may be attributable to a natural insistence upon the unity of truth. But truth . . . may not always be reducible to a single dimension. To see the wholeness of truth we may need to see the obverse side to that aspect which we can [more easily] see, and contain the two aspects in paradoxical tension.
>
> (Casement 1963: 8)

What has since fascinated and concerned me is the discovery that psychoanalysts too can get caught up in this search for certainty, and in the tendency to regard their own dogma as the criterion by which the views of all others should be assessed: those who disagree are then assumed to be in error. Not all of the divisions between schools of psychoanalysis are because one school has a truth that another has not; some of these dogmatic differences derive from the persisting belief that truth can be defined and will prove to be unified. Truth is bound to be more complex. But we cannot always stand, or understand, it being so.

Polarization and schism inevitably follow from any dogmatic claim to the singular correctness of one's own views, and these tendencies abound in quite different spheres of life: in religion, in politics, and in psychoanalysis. It has also interested me to find that, even though psychoanalysis espouses the open-mindedness of anthropology, and is suspicious of religious belief as the illusion that it may be, some psychoanalysts defend their chosen dogma with nothing short of a religious fervour. And sometimes they expect others to have the open minds that they do not always manage to sustain within themselves.

For years now I have held to a questioning agnosticism – unburdened by the 'certainty' of either the believer or the committed atheist. My first attempt at articulating this was in an article entitled 'False security?'. I tried to warn against the seductiveness of certainty, which (I now realize) applies as much to analysts in relation to their chosen 'gods' as to any religious person. In that article I say:

> We must search our hearts, be ready to be stripped of any comfort in believing, and be prepared to look beyond our idea of God lest it be no more than our own projection. . . . Faith must know that it can never know, and must be aware of the guile of its own need to believe.
>
> (Casement 1964: 30)

In relation to psychoanalysis, I would wish now to add that dogmatic certainty will always constrict an analyst's capacity to think imaginatively about the patient. It also constricts the analytic space, without which (as I intend to show in Chapter 10) patients cannot grow most fully into the richness of their own creative potential.

Understanding theory through experience

When (during my social work training) I was first required to learn about unconscious processes and psychodynamic theory, I remained very sceptical about all of this. Too much seemed to be taken for granted – without (I thought) sufficient evidence to support it. However, when I started seeing social work clients I began to discover my own clinical data; and bits of analytic theory did begin to make some sense. But I still could not accept the idea of interpreting to a client/patient on the basis of theory alone. The anthropologist in me rebelled against putting ideas into someone else's mind. (This reluctance shows most clearly in my work with a child that I describe in Chapter 3.) I therefore preferred to discover with clients and patients – in their own terms – what made sense to them. Even though it might take longer this way, I felt that such meaning as could be found made more sense to a client/patient if I did not insist upon taking the short-cut of applying theory too directly.

Learning about transference and countertransference

Having developed a resistance to dogmatism I naturally had difficulty with some of the more extreme attitudes that I came across in the course of my training in psychotherapy, and later in psychoanalysis. For instance, I could not accept that everything said by a patient necessarily represented unconscious communication, or that the process of every session was determined by patients transferring past attitudes on to the analyst. So, how could one justify the technique of interpreting everything in terms of the transference? This seemed to me to be a convenient way for therapists and analysts to ignore those elements of a patient's communication that could be directly about themselves and might sometimes be all too accurate.

I began to feel that the external realities in the analytic relationship should also be taken into account. Here we will often find what has triggered a transference reaction – because of a similarity between an element of present reality and some key experience in the patient's past. The patient then treats this element in the present as if it were the same as something experienced before. But, it should be remembered, that current reality is not always external: it can also be a sense of similarity (to something from the past) that is created through what the patient is *feeling*; this too can lead into a transference experience.

The above view of transference helped me to see it as more understandable – to myself and to the patient – because less mysterious in how it comes about (see Casement 1985: ch. 1). And the purpose in these transference responses, which emerges through trying to understand them, eventually led me to think that transference could also be thought of as an expression of 'unconscious hope' by which the patient signals to the external world that there is conflict needing attention.

For a long time after I had trained as a psychotherapist I questioned the use that some people made of such concepts as countertransference and projective identification.

Countertransference had acquired many different meanings (see Casement 1985: 92–5) and, even in the 1970s, some analysts still seemed to regard any affective response to the patient as evidence of something unresolved in the mind of the analyst/ therapist: a transference to the patient of some emotional significance that belonged elsewhere in the therapist's own past experience – not therefore to be confused with any communication from the patient. But sometimes, it seemed to me, a therapist was being unconsciously prompted by the patient *to become like* the person with whom the patient was reliving earlier difficulties. If that were so, then I believed it necessary to postulate a distinction between 'personal countertransference' (what has to do with the therapist) and 'diagnostic response' – that indicates something about the patient (Casement 1973).

It was several years later that Sandler gave us the notion of unconscious role-responsiveness, through which the patient unconsciously prods the analyst to 'actualize' a key object-relationship from the patient's earlier life (Sandler 1976). Pearl King added a further perspective on the patient's impact upon the analyst in her paper 'Affective response of the analyst to the patient's communications', pointing out how a patient sometimes places the analyst in the role of victim whilst the patient acts out an identification with the aggressor – thereby communicating to the analyst something of the patient's own earlier experience of having been treated in ways similar to how the patient is now treating the analyst (King 1978). I believe that these particular writings have greatly helped to clarify what many analysts and therapists had found in their clinical work without having had an authoritative explanation to support their intuitive impressions. Such is the process of learning from the patient.

Projective identification was even more difficult for me to understand.[2] How did this communication come about, and how could one make interpretive use of it without seeming to understand the patient magically? (I had never been able to accept interpretations being given to patients that seemed to be based solely upon the therapist's feelings about the patient.) I began to understand this process only when I had the experience of being in the presence of a patient whose absence of appropriate feelings had been deeply affecting me: I then realized that I had been picking up a sense of the patient's unshed tears which, for years, she had regarded as too much for her to bear (see Casement 1985: 77–80). Only then could I see that it was through her blank manner of telling me about her babies both dying that she was unconsciously communicating to me those feelings she could not manage within herself alone. I then began to understand what was meant by projective identification and why it can be such an important (and powerful) form of communication. (I return in Chapter 4 to discuss the technical issues involved in interpreting from what the analyst is feeling.)

Discovering the value of trial identification

In the chapter on 'The internal supervisor' (1985: ch. 2) I write of
my experience of working (as a social worker) with someone in a
near-catatonic withdrawal. I illustrate there how it was useful to
imagine myself in the shoes of the other person in order to
monitor how he/she may be experiencing the session and the
therapeutic relationship. I then changed how I was trying to
relate to the patient: no longer trying to get *into* his mind but
beginning to appreciate why he had so much needed to keep me
(and everyone else) *out*. Encouraged by that particular patient's
dramatic response to my new approach to the problem of
communicating with him, I began to explore other ways in which
we can 'trial-identify' with the patient – and the value of it. Since
then I have also found this type of self-monitoring to be useful in
sifting out what we might say in a session from what we do not
say.

The need for an internal supervisor

I learned a lot else too, whilst I was still a social worker, that I
later adopted in my subsequent work as a psychotherapist and
analyst. For example, when supervising social workers, it came to
my notice that (all too often) something I had said by way of
comment or suggestion would be relayed to a client in the next
interview – not always appropriately. This borrowed thinking did
not properly belong to the process going on between the social
worker and the client, but was a left-over from what had been
happening between the social worker and the supervisor.
Something more directly related to what was currently happening
was clearly needed. I therefore began to advise supervisees that
they should aim to establish their own process of supervision (an
internal supervisor) that could help to guide them when in the
presence of the client or patient (see Casement 1985: ch. 2; also
Chapter 9 below, where I discuss more fully the development of
this process of internal supervision).

An internal supervisor is *not* an internalized supervisor: these
are different kinds of resource for the therapist (or analyst).
Drawing upon an internalized supervisor means using someone
else's thinking that may then tend to be superimposed upon what
is happening in the session. Instead of facilitating the analytic
process this will often impede it. By contrast, internal supervision
– being more autonomous – can help us to respond to the

immediacy of the present moment in a session, in ways that are more appropriate to it.

Discovering the value of not-knowing

On one occasion, whilst I was still supervising social workers, I found a student frantically reading up about marital therapy in preparation for his first meeting with a couple who were seeking help with their marriage. I advised him that it is 'all right not to know – and to find out with the client'.

For some time I continued to regard this formula as appropriate advice for students, because they could not yet be expected to know everything: I was then thinking of this as 'permissible ignorance'. It only later began to dawn on me that therapeutic skill does not depend upon knowledge as opposed to ignorance. Rather, there is an important difference between the attempt to understand something from a position of not-knowing and the tendency to prompt, or to direct, which goes with knowing too well. Gradually, therefore, I came to realize that there is real value in keeping to one side what we think we know, in order to leave room for fresh understanding. I then found that Bion had advocated starting every session 'without memory, desire or understanding' – his antidote to those intrusive influences that otherwise threaten to distort the analytic process (Bion 1967a; 1970: 45–54).

I have come to understand this saying of Bion to mean that he was warning against such interferences as: the over-active use of what is remembered from an earlier session (or from the patient's history), the wish to find evidence to support a particular view of the patient (often dictated by theory) or even the wish to make the patient better in a particular way, and the attempt at understanding the patient of today in any way that is not found within the session of today. I have found Bion's advice most helpful in preserving the analytic space from such avoidable impingements and the analytic process from influences that will distort it.

Beyond 'corrective emotional experience'

When I began to train as a psychotherapist I came to think that, in effect, what we might be providing for our patients was a 'corrective emotional experience' – as outlined by Alexander (1954). Clinical experience has gradually made me realize that this is far from the case.

Of course, we do try to offer a reliability that may well be better than patients had previously experienced. But we also provide a freedom for patients to use us in whatever ways belong to their own experience; and we are by no means always put in the role of the 'better parent'. Instead, our patients frequently demonstrate a need to use the analyst to represent earlier 'bad objects'. They can then get in touch with the feelings that could not be expressed (or worked through) with the original object(s). My experience with a patient I describe in the previous volume (1985: ch. 7) taught me very clearly the difference between trying to be a better parent and being used by the patient to represent *traumatic experience as it had been*.

Following the patient

Donald Winnicott, more than any other analyst known to me, was able to remain close to clinical experience, even when writing about theory. And, when I did not at first understand his more difficult papers, I often had the surprise of discovering that I had later stumbled upon what he had been writing about in my own clinical work. I was therefore naturally drawn to his ways of thinking about psychoanalytic experience.

There are some clear examples of re-finding Winnicott in my earlier clinical chapters (1985: chs 5, 7, and 9). Repeatedly I had to struggle with what was immediately present, in whatever way I could. Only afterwards was I able to recognize where I had been. This was especially true when I had been involved in a sequence during which the patient had been using my mistakes to represent earlier 'environmental failure' as described by Winnicott (1965: 258–9). It was in my work with a patient I discuss in the previous volume (1985: ch. 5) that I first recognized this link between my own 'failure' (mistakes I was making at a time when I was trying most particularly not to fail her) and environmental failure in her early life. That patient was then able to direct at me, most powerfully, the feelings which had belonged to those early experiences of trauma.

Another most valuable thing I learned from Winnicott is the value of playing (see Winnicott 1971). This has prompted me to 'play' with clinical material, in supervision or in clinical seminars, and to explore the different meanings that are potentially present within a session.

I have also found it helpful to play with some of Winnicott's own ideas, and to use them differently. For instance, I think of the *analyst's presence* as being potentially available – like the spatula – to be found and to be used in whatever way belongs to the patient at that particular moment.[3]

Likewise, I believe that the transference experience is more convincing when a patient has really been allowed time to invest the analyst with transference significance. The analyst can then be discovered, as an object that has become meaningful to the patient, in the patient's own way and the patient's own time. However, some transference interpretations do seem to be given by the analyst as if these were being pushed down the patient's throat, like a spatula being used (as originally designed) by a forceful physician. It is almost as if this were thought to be what the transference interpretation had been designed for!

As for interpretation in general, I have found it useful to think of Winnicott's 'squiggle game' in his child consultations (Winnicott 1958: ch. 9). He would draw a shape and invite the child to make something of it; or, conversely, the child would draw a shape for Winnicott to do something with. I believe that there is an important place for these incomplete 'shapes' in our work with patients; and this is what has led me to think of offering a *halfway step to interpretation* – for the patient to do something with – rather than the analyst monopolizing insight in a session.

There are many other parallels between Winnicott's clinical observations and my own work, and it is to him that I am most indebted.

Mutuality between patient and analyst

I have already given some references (above) to some of the writings on the unconscious interactions between analyst and patient (e.g. Sandler and King). In addition, I was much influenced by the earlier writings of those other British analysts who had already drawn attention to an unconscious mutuality between patient and analyst. For instance, Paula Heimann had said: 'The analyst's countertransference is not only part and parcel of the analytic relationship, but it is the patient's *creation*, it is part of the patient's personality' (Heimann 1950: 83). And Margaret Little introduces yet another quite new idea: 'We often hear of the mirror which the analyst holds up to the patient, but the patient holds one up to the analyst too' (Little 1951: 37). This brings us back to the importance of the analyst becoming aware of his/her own contribution to the analytic encounter and the need to monitor the effects of this on the analytic process.

British analysts (and many others from abroad) have been deeply influenced by the work and teaching of Rosenfeld who increasingly focused upon the analyst's contribution to what was happening in the analysis – in particular in the event of analyst and patient getting into an impasse (Rosenfeld 1987). This view of the analytic relationship has long been acknowledged in the clinical practice of British analysts even though it was never systematized (except recently by Rosenfeld) in any way comparable to the comprehensive development of an interactional viewpoint *per se* that is found in the writings of Langs.

Resisting dogmatic certainty

When I first read one of Langs' books, *The Listening Process* (1978), I recognized many parallels between his way of working and what I had been evolving over the previous ten years. For a while, therefore, I tried (albeit rather self-consciously) to apply his ways of thinking to my clinical work, and I give examples of that endeavour in the earlier volume (1985: chs 3 and 5). But I began to feel uncomfortable about the incisiveness with which Langs evaluates the clinical work of others. It appears as if he thinks that there is only one right way of working analytically. Ironically, I am now sure that it was precisely the dogmatic certainty of his approach that had first attracted me (without my realizing it) to Langs' views – and it was this also that later turned me away from his own use of them.

I began to understand there was something wrong here, for me at least, when I noticed that my own internal supervision was becoming self-persecutory (see Casement 1985: chs 3 and 5). This amounted to a resurgence of an *internalized supervisor*, which was contrary to the style of work I had been developing before, and it prompted me to realize that my readiness to adopt some of Langs' sureness showed a regressive manifestation of my own earlier wish for dogmatic certainty.

It was inevitable, therefore, that I later moved away from the influence of Langs. Nevertheless, despite these points of disagreement, I readily acknowledge my indebtedness to him in the earlier volume; and I still regard his concept of 'unconscious supervision by the patient' (an imaginative extension of Little's notion of the patient as mirror) as one of the most productive new insights into psychoanalytic technique that has come to light in recent years.

In the rest of my earlier volume (and in this) I try to show a more playful use of internal supervision, wanting to create the atmosphere of a sandpit (playing with different shapes) rather than that of a court-room; but a continuing tension between these two attitudes is still evident in the first book. Outgrowing a longstanding wish to be more sure can only be achieved gradually and with difficulty.

Remaining an independent analyst[4]

It has been interesting to find that a number of reviewers of my first book felt it necessary to locate the author theoretically. As a result, I was variously labelled as a 'disciple of Winnicott', 'a pupil of Bion', or as 'primarily indebted to Langs'; and why am I not a self psychologist? This probably reflects my training as a member of the independent group of the British Psycho-Analytical Society. From that position, in a society which has been able to hold together differing viewpoints within a creative tension, it was possible for me to draw upon whichever ideas have most helped to develop my clinical work. My interest therefore has come to focus upon the patient, and what makes sense with a particular patient in a given session, rather than upon any one theoretical position. I think that this more open-minded approach to clinical work is not easy for everyone to stomach, particularly for those who closely identify themselves with one school of psychoanalysis as *opposed* to others.

Because of this insistence upon an open-minded approach to understanding the individual, one of the criticisms levelled at the independent psychoanalysts in the British Society is that they are said to be 'woolly minded'. However, J. B. Priestley had his own strong views on what some people choose to call 'woolly mindedness':

> Both the fanatical believers and the fixed-attitude people are loud in their scorn of what they call 'woolly minds'. I have defended woolly minds before, and will now do so again. It is the woolly mind that combines scepticism of everything with credulity about everything. Being woolly it has no hard edges. It is easy, pliant, yet it has its own toughness. Because it bends, it does not break. . . . The woolly mind realizes that we live in an unimaginable gigantic, complicated, mysterious universe. To try to stuff the vast bewildering creation into a few neat pigeon-holes is absurd. We don't know enough, and to pretend we do is mere intellectual conceit. (Almost all men who like to refer scornfully to woolly minds suffer from this conceit.) The best we can do is to keep looking out for clues, for

anything that will light us a step or two into the dark. . . . The woolly mind can be silly at times, but even so, it finds out more and enjoys more than the rat-trap intelligence. Second-rate scientists are never woolly-minded whereas great scientists let their minds go woolly between experiments.

(Priestley 1972: 30–1)

Some other reactions to volume one

Some regret has been expressed that I did not give a fuller theoretical framework. But in neither volume have I been trying to write a book that would be complete in itself. Each is intended to be accessible to a wider readership than a more theoretical book would be. I therefore rely upon the reader either being familiar with the theoretical frames that I refer to, or take for granted, or upon the reader's readiness to seek a fuller description of these elsewhere.

It also seems that, in volume one, I did not make it clear at which level I think the process of internal supervision takes place. For instance, do I really wish to suggest that it should all be at a conscious level – as it would appear from some examples I gave in the text? No! I would wish to advocate something more nearly preconscious; but the act of writing about it inevitably shifts the focus away from the more subliminal level at which this process most usually needs to function.

I offered *On Learning from the Patient* as a series of statements about clinical issues that I believe to be important, but I chose to leave them incomplete – rather like Winnicott's squiggles. These were for others to interact with, to complete in their own ways or to challenge, according to their own thinking and experience. I therefore made no attempt there to resolve the dissonances between established theory and some of the therapeutic practices that I described. Instead, I left evidence around in that volume (as I shall in this) of a continuing tussle within myself on both clinical and theoretical issues.

I make no apology for leaving the reader with some continuing uncertainty, as I regard this to be an essential basis for a healthy questioning of what analysts and therapists are trying to do. I also believe that psychotherapy students and others can be better helped in discovering that they are not alone in being so much less than certain in their own clinical work. This conflict, between a search for certainty and a need to remain open to the experience of still not-knowing, can become the source of a patient's greatest potential for change and creativity.

The present volume describes further clinical encounters in which individuals wrestle to become free from the influences of the past – helped by the analytic process, which (when followed) can lead both analyst and patient towards what the patient most needs to find in the course of the analytic encounter.

Chapter two

Interpretation: fresh insight or cliché?[1]

In this chapter I try to show how a too dogmatic application of analytic interpretation can become absurd or sterile. There are times when it is more fruitful to work in a way that leaves room for insight to become a genuine experience of discovery, for the analyst as well as for the patient.

When we find ourselves using similar forms of interpretation with several different patients, it is probable that we are becoming stereotyped and repetitive. And when this repetition develops into cliché interpreting, it is likely to promote an intellectualization of the analytic experience. How then can we recover that freshness of insight which alone can promote therapeutic change?

Typical examples of cliché interpretation might be: 'You are really talking about me'; 'You are seeing me as your mother'; 'You are experiencing separation anxiety'; 'You are rendering me impotent'; 'You are experiencing castration anxiety'; 'You are making envious attacks upon my understanding'. Examples like these are common in the analytic literature, which makes me wonder how frequently they may be used in the consulting-room.

We cannot always avoid interpreting in ways that have been frequently used before (by others or by ourselves) but the effectiveness of such interpretations is easily dulled through overuse. Also, when we rely on what has come to be regarded as universal truths, we can lose touch with the individual. Therefore, when some stereotyped interpretation is foremost in our thinking, it is often better to delay before speaking and to look for some less focused comment that can lead towards subsequent interpretation. The patient will frequently lead us to insight that is more specific and often quite new.

Example 2.1

I once pointed out to a patient a recurring theme that he, as a child and since, had become preoccupied with protecting his penis against some expected hurt or threat. (The interpretation that I was not making is quite obvious here.) He replied: 'I am afraid of it being broken off.' Let us notice how much more telling is his own description of castration anxiety. The threat was not just to the penis but to the excited penis. It cannot be thought of as being broken off unless it is erect.

I am not thinking only of the danger that actual interpretations become clichés because of their familiar form. I am also concerned with the stereotyped thinking that engenders this: for instance, the notion that everything in a session should be interpreted in terms of the transference, or in terms of the patient's current regression in the transference relationship. The danger then is that we will notice only what our theoretical assumptions prompt us to look for, and our preconceptions begin to be imposed upon what we see.

I came across a salutary warning of this, when I was reading anthropology, in a book about the sexual symbolism of musical instruments. The author, captivated by his reading of Freud, argued that every musical instrument is symbolically male or female. Having got carried away by the shape of violins and cellos he noticed that they are played on with long thin things called bows. These, he claimed, are phallic symbols. He then proceeded to go through the entire orchestra; and how could anyone argue with him?

He pointed out all those other long thin instruments that people put into their mouths; the shape of those wooden drum-sticks; and those other drum-sticks with large woolly balls; and, what's more, these drum-sticks are beaten against the stretched skin of the drums, which (he said) represents the hymen. And what about those inviting hollows at the end of all the brass instruments; and the triangle, which is set ringing by a very small phallic symbol? And so on! After reading all of this, some joker had written in the margin: 'If Sir Malcolm Sargent knew what is really going on in front of him, and what he is waving around in his own hand, he would never conduct another concert!'

What I am trying to illustrate in this caricature of analytic interpretation is that, when any psychoanalytic assumption is held to be beyond question, interpretations can too easily be imposed upon whatever appears to fit in with that assumption. Clinically, we must always be wary of this tendency to think that we are seeing evidence of what we are expecting to find, particularly as we are all inclined to relate to the familiar as if it were universal.

I would like to suggest that some of our stereotyped thinking is due to a mistaken response to the patient's communications. This response could be described as a *transferential attitude to elements of the clinical situation* (Casement 1985: 9–12). In ways similar to the processes of transference, we can find ourselves responding to a patient in terms of our familiarity with analytic theory or other clinical experience. We then transfer on to the patient the understanding that we have gleaned elsewhere, even though it may not apply to this particular patient.[2] This is what I mean by cliché-thinking.

I believe that we are most likely to engage in these repetitive forms of interpreting when we feel insecure about our clinical understanding. By prematurely imagining that we recognize what the patient is communicating, even if we don't, we can preserve the appearance (at least to ourselves) of being competent. There is then a danger that we interpret on the basis of similarity rather than from a more genuine process of analytic discovery.

The pitfalls of preconception are a hazard not only for the novice. A similar danger lies in wait for the experienced therapist. The authority of experience can tempt the practitioner to become lazy in his thinking, or too sure. And it is often tempting to use short-cuts to insight, based upon what has already made sense with other patients.

In the following vignette I was fortunate that my patient prompted me to reorientate my thinking.

Example 2.2

In a session some time during the first year of analysis, a patient began to be distressed about her hair going grey. At first I thought I was hearing about vanity, particularly when I noticed that I could not see grey hairs. I tried looking closer, peering over the back of the couch, but I still couldn't see any grey. However, when I wondered about this shift in my position – from sitting normally in my chair to leaning towards the patient – I thought that I was being manoeuvred into getting physically closer to her. I therefore mistook this interaction to be evidence of some hysterical manipulation.

When I interpreted this as the patient trying to get me to be closer to her, she became much more distressed. She began crying from deep inside herself. Only then did I recognize that the patient had been trying to tell me about how she felt inside herself, where the scars of her childhood experiences made her

feel that she was growing prematurely old. Part of the problem
was that her emotional scars were not visible – and yet she
needed me to be aware of them.[3]

My reorientation here was possible only when I recognized that
the patient's response to my first interpretation was not due to
resistance, as I had been tempted to think. Her increased distress
contained an unconscious cue for me to listen to the deeper
meaning in her communication. She needed me to be prepared to
be in touch with the pain of her *internal* world.

In my initial failure to look beneath the surface appearance, I
had become like her mother. The patient then felt left alone with
her distress, as she had been as a child. But, through a
reorientation of my listening, I was able to arrive at a quite
different understanding of this sequence. Moreover, the patient
was also able to discover that her capacity to cue the other person
had not after all been lost to her for ever. That is how it had
seemed to her after she had been badly burned at the age of
eleven months. After that trauma her mother had seemed to be
no longer able to respond to her inner pain; she had concentrated
instead on the healing of the external scars from the burning.

It is not easy for a patient to question, let alone to reorientate,
the therapist unless the patient is unusually tenacious – as with
the patient I have just described. So, what happens if we let
ourselves become dogmatic in our interpreting? One thing at
least is certain: that we will become less receptive to correction
from a patient.

Also, let us wonder what is happening when our theoretical
orientation becomes obtrusively evident in what we are saying to
a patient. Are we imposing our theory upon what we are
hearing? I think of this as 'jelly-moulding', giving a shape to
clinical material that does not inherently belong to it.

The next example comes from the work of a foreign colleague. I
think that the style of interpreting here would be described as
a caricature. Similar caricatures can be found in all schools of
psychoanalysis.

Example 2.3

At a clinical workshop I heard a case presentation given by a
therapist who is bilingual, in English and the language of her
mother-tongue. The patient she described is a man whom she
had been seeing in three-times-a-week therapy. The sessions
were reported in English but the therapy was being conducted
in the patient's own language.

It was soon evident that this therapist's style of work is one of quite unusual sureness about her understanding of the patient. Then, in one session that was described in detail, the patient reported a dream. He said: 'I had a dream last night in which my head was being squashed by someone sitting on my face.'

What followed, after the patient had failed to free associate, was a product of the therapist's silent working over of this dream in the context of her assumptions about the patient's state of regression in the therapy. He was regarded as still at the breast. But in the dream, where there should have been a mouth/breast relationship, there was a face pressed against buttocks. The therapist was therefore able to argue to herself that this must have been derived from a distortion of the feeding relationship. She therefore offered the following interpretation: 'Because of your envy, you are unable to take in the good milk of my interpretations. Instead you take in my words as poisonous faeces.'

The patient's response to this interpretation was to remain silent, and then to appear to change the subject. He eventually came out of his silence with the following statement: 'I am going to America for my holiday, but I don't speak English. This will make me very vulnerable because it means that I will have to be totally dependent on my wife to explain to me everything that is being said.' The therapist then proceeded to interpret the patient's separation anxiety.

This material was from sessions during the month prior to a summer break, so it was not surprising to hear the therapist refer to reactions to separation when the patient had spoken about his summer holiday. Indeed, at some level, these interpretations may have had their own truth. But what if the patient is not simply regressed to an infant/breast relationship? What if the patient is also responding to the therapist's style of working? We might be hearing examples of *unconscious supervision by the patient* (Langs 1978).

If we go over the material once more, using trial identification with the patient to help us to look at *the patient's view of the therapist*, we gain a different position from which to listen to this interaction.

The patient may be feeling battered by his over-sure therapist. If so, the dream might allude to the experience of not being allowed his own thoughts. Someone was squashing the patient's head – perhaps making thinking impossible. It could therefore be an unconscious prompt to the therapist to reconsider her dogmatic way of interpreting.

The therapist, however, seems to be unaware of any prompting by the patient. She proceeds to interpret this dream no less dogmatically; and she regards the ensuing silence to be an acceptance by him of the interpretation. She also assumes that the change of subject has been determined by the impending holiday break. Her interpretations therefore seem to be super-imposed upon what the patient is saying: they do not develop from within the session itself.

Let us again trial-identify with the patient. Where does the notion of 'poisonous faeces' come from in this session? Surely not out of the patient's own thinking but from the therapist's theoretical orientation. Maybe, then, the patient's next statements are more directly related to this interpretation. As well as referring to the holiday break, the patient could be saying: 'I can't understand your language. If you can't use mine it could make me totally dependent upon you to explain to me what you are saying.'

The communication here is, of course, bound to be over-determined – having several levels of meaning at the same time. We may also be hearing references to the transference, in that we know the therapist to be fluent in more than one language and it is quite likely that the patient knows that too.

Holiday breaks are one of many stimuli for cliché interpretations. We might consider some other clinical phenomena that can trigger what I am calling here a transferential attitude to familiar clinical experience.

Lateness may be an expression of resistance, or of some angry feelings towards the therapist. But it can be other things too. For instance, it is sometimes a token bid for the session to start in the patient's own time – not the therapist's. And that does not always have to be seen in terms of a wish to control the therapist. Patients quite often endeavour to 'own' the analytic space, and the time of a session; and it is important that they can find ways to establish this as truly theirs. Too often, lateness is listened to only for its negative connotations.

This may also apply to *silence*. We encounter many different kinds of silence in the clinical setting, but some therapists are prone to fall back upon stereotyped thinking when trying to deal with prolonged silences. One of these stereotypes is to hold too strongly to the notion that the patient should always be left to speak first. There are occasions when we need to recognize that the *patient has already started the session* – with silence. We are less likely to get into a sterile game of waiting if we learn to 'read' a patient's silence, and sometimes to respond tentatively to what we sense as the underlying communication which is being conveyed in this. Silence does not always have to be withholding or resisting.

A similar stalemate sometimes develops around the issue of a patient's *anger*. Not infrequently we notice that a patient has difficulty in expressing anger – particularly in the session. It is then talked about as something that happens only outside the consulting-room, or as something that seems not to happen at all because of the patient's inhibition of anger.

Example 2.4

One therapist, whom I supervised, quite often interpreted the *absence of anger* in her patient's life – as paralleled in her relationship to the therapist. It was known that, throughout her life, the patient had been unable to give expression to her angry feelings; and this could be understood as an inhibition linked with her mother's frequent absences in hospital, and her eventual death when the patient was not yet four years old. Maybe she was afraid that her therapist would be harmed, even killed, by the murderous anger that still brooded in the patient's unconscious, most particularly towards those upon whom she depended and who were too often absent when she needed them.

Gradually the patient began to agree with her therapist that it would be a relief if she could let herself be angry in her sessions; and she had a lot to be angry about. The therapist was of course absent between sessions, and away for holidays. And these absences were experienced by the patient as a desertion of her by the therapist, as by the mother who had often been away in hospital – and who then had died.[4]

In supervision I began to hear details of how this therapist felt in response to the patient's frequent lateness and occasional missing of sessions, and her regular silences at the beginning of every session. I had, in fact, encouraged the therapist to make a point of *starting every session on time with or without the patient*. In this way she came to be most directly exposed to the impact of the patient's various kinds of absence. The therapist had then noticed that she felt badly treated by the patient. She sometimes felt abandoned; or she felt suspended in a state of not knowing where the patient was in a session whilst she remained in prolonged silences; or not knowing what had happened to her patient when she missed a session without telephoning.

Out of this monitoring of the therapist's responses to these silences, or absences, it began to become clear that we had been missing an important point. It was far from true that the patient was unable to express her anger in the sessions. She was doing this nearly all the time – *but it was not being recognized as anger*.

It then began to be possible to rethink the communication conveyed in the unconscious interaction here between this patient and her therapist; and it seemed possible that the therapist was being unconsciously tested to see if she could be aware of the murderous anger being expressed in this behaviour.

Surviving that silent aggression unwittingly, whilst speaking of the absence of the patient's anger in sessions, may therefore have been experienced by the patient as evidence that the therapist was actually afraid of her anger – and that she was unconsciously retreating from this by not letting herself be aware of it. This was exactly how adults had responded to her when she was a child. They too had not been able to cope with her angry feelings – around the time of her mother's death and after it. She had eventually been sent away to a children's home when nobody felt able to manage this distressed child, who had also become very withdrawn. Important changes in the therapy grew out of this new awareness that the patient's anger had been in the session all along, and particularly during her absence.

In this example we can see a shift from cliché-thinking to fresh insight. Silences and absences had been mistaken for resistance. But these could be understood quite differently once the therapist had begun to monitor her affective responses to the patient. It then became possible to see that the patient was 'communicating by impact' (Casement 1985: ch. 4). She was evoking in the therapist, by means of projective identification, a resonance to her own difficult feelings, which she could not communicate in other ways. The therapist could thereby begin to recognize important aspects of the patient's own unmanageable experiences, such as being confronted by her mother's unexplained absences, and not knowing where she was or what was happening to her. But a reorientation in listening had been necessary before this understanding of the patient's non-verbal communication became possible.

As an exercise in differentiating between clinically similar situations, I shall describe a case in which I too was having to struggle with silences in a session.

Example 2.5

A patient (whom I shall call Mrs D) would frequently fall into silences during which she was in evident distress. But when I tried to interpret from my own reading of her distress (in the way I have just been suggesting) it didn't help. Equally, if I left her in silence, that didn't help. Either way she experienced me as putting her under a pressure to speak; and I experienced myself as being in a double-bind.[5] Whatever I did was wrong.

One day the patient stammered out of her silence: 'I am sorry, but I can't help being difficult like this.' She was now experiencing a pressure to apologize. But she was also prompting me to look at her distressed silence differently. I was hearing about something called 'being difficult'. I took this as an unconscious cue.

I was reminded by this that Mrs D's mother would often accuse her of 'being difficult'. She had previously told me that, when she was upset as a child, she could never speak to her mother about what she was feeling. Her mother used to regard this reluctance to speak as perverse and would accuse her of 'being difficult'. But if Mrs D then tried to speak about what she was feeling her mother would turn away from her, saying that she was 'now being impossible'. Her mother could not bear being made to feel upset, as a result of which the patient was made to feel that she was always in the wrong. I had already been aware of this double-binding by the mother. But in this session I was able to hear the patient in a new way.

I replied: 'Perhaps it is precisely this difficulty, in communicating what you are feeling, that you need to convey to me now; but you expect me not to be prepared to stay with you if I actually experience some of that difficulty, so you feel that you must apologize.'

The patient then told me more about her fear of being upset in the presence of her mother. She had frequently been rejected by her for expecting emotional help which was not forthcoming. To avoid this she would shut herself away in her bedroom, in despair of ever finding help with her distress.

Mrs D had to find out whether I could bear to be affected by her difficulty in communicating, without finding her 'impossible'. She also needed to discover whether I could recognize, and find ways of dealing with, her experience of being double-bound; and she had been able to communicate this by double-binding me.

Patients, as well as therapists, may use their familiarity with analytic theory to fall into cliché-thinking, and this will be just as detrimental to real insight. In these situations much of what we might normally be able to say to a patient, without it sounding stereotyped, is heard as cliché by the patient who then says: 'Oh, I thought you would say that.' Other patients seize upon any stereotyped interpretation to further their intellectualization of the analytic process. In either case real experience in the analysis is warded off.

In the following example the patient was constantly ready to make a defensive use of any predictable insight.

Example 2.6

Mrs E came to me for therapy when she was nearly thirty. She had a long history of depression, and now her second marriage was in a state of breakdown. She was analytically sophisticated, anticipating much of what I interpreted to her in the early months of her therapy with me. (She had previously been in treatment with a psychiatrist who seems to have been prone to giving her 'wild' analytic interpretations.)

This patient, born in a Mediterranean country, had been brought up as a Roman Catholic. She first married when she was seventeen. After three years her husband left her, accusing her of frigidity. She felt guilty about sex without knowing why, and she told me that her head would become 'filled with accusing nuns' if ever she began to enjoy sex.

After her first husband had left her she became promiscuous, and began to think of herself as no better than a prostitute. Subsequently she married a much older man. But she so often provoked him to jealousy, by flirting with other men, that he too was threatening to leave. She now felt that she could not stop herself being sexual towards any man who interested her.

Her history revealed an alarming degree of self-destructiveness. This included a car crash from which she had nearly died. Intermittently she had been actively preoccupied with thoughts of suicide. She had also had two abortions. Her relationships with each member of her family were difficult. From early adolescence her father used to beat her, or shut her up in her room, if she ever showed interest in boys. Her mother was also fiercely critical of her. She had a brother four years younger than herself of whom she was intensely jealous.

Much of the detail of this patient's history lent itself readily to a familiar theoretical formulation. For example: I could postulate that Mrs E had been Oedipally attached to her father, particularly looking to him for love when her mother turned to the new baby; that she felt a fierce rivalry from her mother; that her persecutory superego (an introjection of this critical mother) was later represented by the accusing nuns; and that she had come to experience her sexuality as bad – to be totally inhibited or punished lest it became uncontrollable. In addition, there was evidence that she tried to deal with this self-destructively, or to get others to punish her in relation to her sexual interest in men. This interaction may well have originated with her father.

However, this was all based on theory or on other clinical experience. It had not yet grown out of my analytic work with this patient. Some of it had been postulated by the patient herself, based on what she had read, thus forestalling a deeper analytic experience. In addition, it was noticeable that Mrs E displayed an excited expectation that I would be interpreting her Oedipus complex, as her psychiatrist used to do. I therefore chose to defer further interpretation of this.

Gradually the patient's own preconceptions began to fade – as I was not exciting her with sexual interpretations. The therapy moved into other areas, with my own theoretical formulations falling into the background of my thinking and listening. And I stopped looking for, or thinking that I saw, the most obvious things that my analytic training had led me to expect.

In the second year of this three-times-a-week therapy Mrs E told me a dream. She said: 'I was in a bathroom with Kojak. There were many baths – side by side in a row.' She had no associations. After a while I commented: 'I don't understand this dream yet, but I do wonder why there were many baths.' (I was trying to help her to free associate without directing her to say more.) Mrs E had no thoughts about this. After a pause I added: 'I wonder if there could be an unconscious metaphor here for some kind of frequency.' (I was thinking aloud about this strange detail in the dream, knowing that I still could not interpret.) She made nothing more of this so we left it.

In a session two weeks later Mrs E said: 'I dreamed about Kojak again last night. He was with me in my parents' bedroom. He was being sexual with me and I was feeling very excited. We were about to get into bed to make love when I woke up.' This time Mrs E freely offered associations to her dream. She recognized the bedroom because this had been in a house where they had lived when she was four. She remembered it well, as her family had lived there during the year that her brother had been born. About Kojak, she said: 'I really fancy that man. He sucks lollipops like a child and yet he is ever so sexy.'

Here, I felt, I should be especially careful not to pre-empt the patient's discovery in what she was beginning to tell me. I therefore looked for a neutral way of providing a half-way step to insight in order to keep her options open. After a pause, I offered the comment: 'I notice that you have recently had two dreams about Kojak.' (At least there was nothing directive about that!)

Mrs E began to wonder about this: 'I think it has something to do with his bald head. It fascinates and excites me – I can't think why.'

I used a form of stereotyped response here; but, fortunately, it did not lead to the intellectualizing reply that it could have done. I said: 'Perhaps Kojak is not the only person with a bald head who has fascinated or excited you.'

'No,' she replied, 'I don't know any bald men – at least not intimately.' After a pause she cried out, in alarm and disbelief: 'My God! it can't be . . . But yes . . . My father!' (Pause.) 'My father used to wear a wig. I only ever saw him without it once, when I was very little. He was asleep and it had slipped off. He was totally bald; and I had completely forgotten that until now.'

Mrs E then poured out a memory that horrified and shocked her. She was in the bathroom with her father. She was four. Her father was playing with her naked upon his lap, when her mother came in. Her mother started screaming, plunging her into the bath and washing her viciously all over. Her mother was screaming at her father (or was it at her?) whilst looking closely at her vagina.

In the following sessions many other details emerged that related to this experience. Mrs E was convinced that her father had actually abused her sexually; and not only on this occasion but frequently before this too. (Perhaps that was what had been alluded to in the dream detail of the many baths.)

I learned that her parents' marriage had collapsed about that time. Her father, she was eventually told, had turned instead to prostitutes. Could that have been why she had later come to identify herself with prostitutes? And her father punishing her, as a teenager, for being sexual; had she been provoking her second husband to treat her in a similar way?

Psychoanalytic theory, in this case, was discovered to be vividly borne out by clinical experience. But, for it to be clinically useful it had to be rediscovered, not merely applied. It would have served only to increase the patient's defences against remembering if I had anticipated this eruption of unconscious memory by interpreting earlier. Instead, I had to preserve the analytic space from my own preconceptions – and hers. Insight, when it was arrived at, was no cliché. It was discovered when the patient was emotionally ready for this; and she could be ready only when she felt analytically secure enough to remember.

What was then necessary in this therapy was a careful working through of this new insight in the transference. During this phase of the therapy, the patient was only gradually able to allow herself to realize that her manner of relating to me was also clearly sexual – as with 'any man who interested her'. For a long time previously she had believed that it was only by her keeping all sexuality isolated from the therapeutic relationship that this had been kept safe. It therefore became an entirely new experience for her to discover that her sexuality could be acknowledged by me without being exploited, that it could be affirmed, not ignored or run away from. Only thus could she begin to see her sexuality as containable and therefore as benign, as neither bad nor destructive.

Conclusion

We do not have to be so quick to use old insights when we can learn to tolerate longer exposure to what we do not yet understand. And, when we do think we recognize something familiar from a patient, we need still to be receptive to that which is different and new.

There is . . .
At best, only a limited value
In the knowledge derived from experience.
The knowledge imposes a pattern, and falsifies,

For the pattern is new in every moment
And every moment is a new and shocking
Valuation of all that we have been.

('East Coker')

. . . Last season's fruit is eaten
And the fullfed beast shall kick the empty pail.
For last year's words belong to last year's language
And next year's words await another voice.

('Little Gidding')
(T.S.Eliot *Four Quartets*)

In psychoanalysis and psychotherapy our task is to find, in the
patient and in ourselves, that other voice.

Chapter three

A child leads the way

A key theme in this volume is that of the unconscious search for what is needed, whereby children and patients give unconscious cues that indicate what they are looking for in key relationships.

My first analytic work of any kind was with a child. From my detailed notes we can follow the process whereby this child gradually prompted me first to provide the therapeutic setting she needed, and then to put into words the anxieties that had been blocking her learning. Eventually she made me overcome my reluctance to interpret, and she began to make significant progress when I did.

Introduction

I have already indicated, in the previous chapter, that one time when therapists are most likely to fall into using the stereotyped thinking of others is when they are feeling insecure about their own clinical understanding. The choice then seems to be either to interpret as others might or to trust in the patient's unconscious to lead the way. But this latter choice presupposes a positive potential in the analytic process which can safely be followed. I was fortunate to have had a chance to see evidence of that potential early in my analytical career.

I am giving an account here of my first five weeks of seeing a child 'patient', aged six and a half. I shall call her Joy. Some alterations of personal detail have been made to preserve the anonymity of the family, but I have not concealed my sense of bewilderment and naivety. What seems to me so extraordinary about this sequence is how Joy managed to communicate her own sense of what she most needed. Of course it also shows the importance of a proper training in child psychotherapy. However, I trust that the reader will be able to share something of the experience of feeling my way until I discovered more clearly what this child needed of me.

I have included all the details that I have of Joy's play so that readers can assess for themselves what may have influenced this clinical sequence. I have also given my reflections, as they were during a session or immediately afterwards when I wrote up my notes. Sometimes I have added retrospective thoughts, in parentheses or as 'comment', but for the most part I leave readers to form their own ideas about what could, or should, have been interpreted. I have therefore not changed or added to my original notes as I believe that it may be more interesting to be able to follow my struggles to understand and to manage what was happening.

The reader will be able to see from this account how Joy persistently prompted me until I made the moves which gave her what she needed. Thus, the reading lessons that her parents wanted her to have gave way to therapy, which she needed; the drawing-room provided for the reading gave place to a play-room; the need for a sufficient privacy from the mother's anxious intrusion was regularly signalled until I acted upon it; the freedom to make mess, as part of the therapy, was increasingly indicated until this was provided. Much more was to follow. This child really did lead the way whilst I had to pluck up my courage to follow.

Referral

I was in my second year as a student on an adult psychotherapy training course when I was asked to see Joy. She was referred to me by her mother's analyst, who recommended that I could be used as a 'reading teacher', and that I might also 'keep an eye on the psychotherapeutic needs' of the child.

I arranged for supervision whilst I was seeing Joy, but I started out with a strong reluctance to accept any interpretive role with her. This was partly because I had not been trained to work with a child in this way but was further fuelled by my recent reading of Klein's account of her work with 'Richard' (Klein 1961).

I had formed an opinion from my reading of 'Richard' that Klein had been providing that child with a symbolic language through which he could, eventually, communicate deep anxiety or unconscious phantasy with a possibility that this could be understood by the person who had been teaching him this language. But my reservations about working in that way were: that it assumed an extraordinary degree of certainty about a child's inner world which I did not have, and I was not sure whether compliant agreement with that certainty could really be distinguished from more autonomous communications that might not be in agreement with it. I also wondered whether Joy would be able to find her own language for communicating to me. I was therefore determined not to pre-empt her thinking with any interpretations that might assume that I knew more of her unconscious than I could be fairly sure of. So I waited for Joy to show me what she needed. I was, however, slow to respond to her increasingly clear demands for a change of setting and for unambiguous therapeutic work because of my own reluctance to be drawn into that.

Fortunately, Joy was not content with anything less than she needed, and from our first meeting she gave me repeated cues to understand that her inability to read was a symptomatic condition: she needed someone to recognize that she was having difficulties about her position in the family as the only girl. Later it also became clear that she did not have the words for her sexual curiosity and anxiety, but she remained healthily determined that I should not fob her off with merely euphemistic acknowledgements of what she was trying to say through her play. She needed to have interpretations spelled out quite directly and, when I was eventually able to help her discover the hidden positives of her female body, she immediately rewarded me by showing how much she had been learning from my attempts to teach her to read.

Family background

Joy was six and a half when I first saw her. She had two brothers – I will call them Richard (aged nine) and Tom (aged two). The referrer had told me that Joy's mother had had difficulty accepting her because she was a girl. Soon after she was born, Joy was handed over to a nanny and there had been minimal physical contact between Joy and her mother since then. I was also told that Joy was over-indulged – that she had been allowed to have and to do much as she pleased. By contrast there was a more openly affectionate relationship between the mother and Joy's brothers, and it was particularly striking how much more physical care Tom was receiving from his mother, who took care of him herself, whilst Joy had been in the care of a series of nannies.

Meeting the parents

I naturally met the parents before I saw Joy. I saw them in their home and they gave me details of her schooling. The father also told me that he saw Joy as 'a very sexual child', and that she was quite seductive towards him. He and Joy had recently begun to spend weekends together at their seaside cottage, where she loved to run up and down the beach playing with him. He explained that he made her special in this way to make up for having been away so much in the past. (His job had frequently taken him abroad.) He said that he rather hoped that Joy would 'fall in love' with me and so learn to read – for me.

The parents said that their poodle, Polo, was very important to Joy, and they had told her that Polo might have puppies in the spring as they had recently taken her to spend a few days with a 'boyfriend poodle'.

It was agreed at this meeting that I would see Joy every weekday morning, for the first week until Christmas, and less frequently thereafter.

Working with Joy

First meeting with Joy (a Tuesday)

I could see Joy only at her home. When I arrived for the first time, her mother showed me into the room that she had allocated for 'the reading lessons'. This was the family drawing-room where, it was suggested, I would be 'least disturbed by other noises and goings-on in the house'. Unfortunately, the room was huge and (for the purposes of any play-therapy) it felt oppressively clean, tidy, and respectable. But because of my ambiguous brief for seeing Joy, I did not feel able to ask for alternative arrangements at this point.

The mother asserted her control from the beginning by coming in with a tray of coffee and biscuits, which she put on a table beside the chair she had designated as mine. Before leaving me alone with Joy, the mother asked me what Joy should call me: 'Patrick' or 'Mr Casement'? I suggested that Joy could decide this for herself after she had got to know me.

I had brought with me a medium-sized, flabby, and well-used 'holdall'. In this there were some felt pens in lots of colours, a scribbling pad, some coloured sticky paper and scissors, some plasticine in various colours, and some remedial reading material.

I asked Joy if she knew why I was there and she replied 'to teach me to read'. I asked her if she wanted to be able to read. 'Part of me does and part of me doesn't', she replied. I asked about the part that *did* want to read: 'I would like to be able to read like Anne', a friend who had moved up to the next form that term when Joy had been left behind. (I realized later that I had not asked about the part of her that did *not* want to read.)

I told Joy that we would be doing some reading games eventually, but first I would like her to play – and I let her explore the contents of my holdall. Joy chose to play with the plasticine. She wanted to make Polo (the family poodle) and chose brown 'because that is Polo's colour'. She made a large fat sausage from which she pinched legs, head, and tail, making quite a skilled model of a dog. I said 'Polo is rather fat isn't she?' and Joy replied 'Well she is going to be fat because she's going to have puppies.' I asked how she knew this. 'Of course she is because she went away to stay with Gonzo; he's a boy poodle, and Mummy and Daddy say that she's going to have puppies.'

Joy made a model of her brother Richard out of red plasticine. 'We'll make him big because he's ever so big – almost as big as you.' I asked her how we could tell that he was a boy. (I wanted to give her permission to be more explicit about sexual differences, because of the apparent discrimination against her by her mother.) She replied: 'Of course you know.' When I asked her to show me, she took more red plasticine and made a long thin sausage. She looked at me mischievously and pressed it flat saying 'That's his school cap.' She pinched this and drew out a long peak. I commented on what a large peak he had and she replied 'Well, that's to keep the sun out of his eyes.' She made another thin sausage, hesitated where to put it, squashed it and made it into his 'satchel'. She made a very thin length of plasticine, again hesitated up and down the body, and then quickly put it on to the satchel. She told me 'That's his big pencil.' Finally she made a tiny lump of plasticine and, after more hesitation and knowing looks, made a quick decision: 'That's his ink pot', and she stuck this on to his satchel too. Richard was made to sit astride Polo but he kept falling off.

Reflection

In this material we can see several issues already emerging. Joy knew about pregnancy. She also knew about sexual differences, having been given a lead from me to be able to acknowledge this, but she was afraid of being explicit. The penis symbols were all eventually disguised – as a peak cap, a satchel, a pencil and an ink pot. There was also some reference to being able to see more clearly, helped by the peaked cap 'to keep the sun out of his eyes'. (This was the first of many references to eyes and seeing.)

There may have been an early indication of transference in Joy speaking of Richard as 'ever so big – almost as big as you'.

Joy then began drawing. She drew her mother first, adding Polo beside her. Then she dotted the picture saying 'It's raining.' She drew her father and added: 'He must have an umbrella – we'll give him one.' She began to draw an umbrella but changed this into 'his brief-case'. 'He doesn't need an umbrella', she said, 'because the sun is shining.' She drew a black radiant sun. Then she drew Richard and Tom.

While Joy was still drawing she looked up to me and said very confidentially: 'I'm going to tell you a secret. You are not to tell anyone.' I asked if this meant that she didn't want her mother to know. '*No-one* must know', she said with great emphasis. (Pause.) 'I have a secret telephone under the chair. I ring up Anne on this whenever I want to, without anyone knowing.' This was the end of the session.

Reflection

I felt that I could see something of Joy's ambivalence towards each of her parents in her drawing of them. In relation to her mother she seemed to wish to be allowed to be special to her – with Polo, the only other female in the family, drawn close to the mother. (Joy had added rain to the picture, and later I learned that she had been persistently enuretic since her mother's pregnancy with Tom had begun to show. She had been dry before then but wet every night since.) I was not sure about her representation of the father, with a black sun shining down on him. In relation to me, I felt that she sounded conspiratorial in telling me her secret – something that must be kept just between her and me. But we may also be seeing an unconscious prompt for me to establish boundaries around her contact with me. With her mother bringing in coffee at the beginning, and hanging around to see me before I left, these boundaries did not yet properly exist.

At the end of the session I thanked the mother for bringing me coffee but added that I would prefer not have this in future 'because it rather gets in the way'.

Session 2 (Wednesday)

During this session Joy drew Polo again but made her very thin. I commented 'You've made her thin today.' Joy said 'She's had her puppies' and drew a red puppy and red rain which fell on both mother and puppy. She added another puppy in blue, dotted the red puppy with blue and added blue rain which drizzled down on the blue puppy.

Reflection

I felt that Joy was representing a wish to be alone with her mother (Polo with one baby, both mother and puppy in red). After she had added another puppy in blue she went back to dot the red puppy with blue, perhaps expressing the wish to have some of the blue colour in herself to make her more like her brother. I wondered about enuresis around the birth of Tom, but I didn't yet know the details of this. I did not interpret any of this to Joy.

Joy drew a gorilla. She said: 'We'll put him on another page because he has big thumbs.' She drew the thumbs. She drew squiggles to make a tree, drew a banana at the top, put a banana in the gorilla's hand and said: 'I like to take bananas when Mummy's not looking.' She drew a hand reaching into the picture from below. I asked her to show me that the gorilla was a man. She covered him over by drawing trousers on him.

Reflection

I felt that Joy was indicating jealousy towards her brothers, and perhaps her father, because they were allowed to have what she would like to have. She had to steal a banana whereas the man gorilla had a banana all to himself. The phallic symbolism of the big thumbs, and the banana, seemed obvious. Again, I made no comment.

I had the impression that Joy was refusing to look at the more visible maleness of her brothers because of the disturbing preference given to them in the family, and because she had not yet discovered a positive view of herself as female. So I invited Joy to show me the maleness of the gorilla, in order to let her know that it was all right for her to acknowledge this more directly. But she couldn't yet dispense with her need to retreat from more direct references to the distinction between the sexes, and she used plenty of other symbols of her own.

Session 3 (Thursday)

During this session Joy remarked: 'You must get rid of that case and get a new one. That one is all dirty.' It seemed that she didn't like the thought that I had taken it with me to see other children. She wanted me to be 'new' with her. The case, however, remained unchanged and she eventually accepted it.

Joy began immediately with drawing. She drew a mound and drew two lines across it, calling it a cave. Beside this she drew a square with wheels. I asked her if this might be a car. 'No.' She drew more wheels and made it into a crane, drawing a large extension up into the sky. She blobbed in the end of this, drew a line coming out of the blob, thought about it and drew another line. From this she dangled a man. 'That's you', she said. She filled in the bottom of the cave with little dots and asked me 'What are those?' I said: 'You tell me.' 'They are treasures and you have to go down into the cave to fetch them out, and here [drawing more] is a rope ladder to help you down, and here [drawing] is Polo standing over the treasures to keep them safe for you, and here to the right [drawing] is a passage – you can escape out of that if you need to.' She drew Gonzo (Polo's mate) standing in this passage 'to help Polo keep everything safe'. She drew a figure half-way up the crane: 'That is Richard who is watching to see that everything is all right.' She drew a large support to keep up the end of the crane. She looked at the picture and was clearly pleased with it.

While drawing this Joy had told me about the gardener, who had recently made a big bonfire and how she had to run away because of all the smoke. Later, whilst she was still drawing, I happened to rub one of my eyes. She stopped drawing and said very earnestly: 'I should have told you – you mustn't rub an itch, because although at first it feels nice it soon begins to hurt.' I noticed the allusion to masturbatory experience but chose not to comment.

My first remark to Joy about her drawing was: 'It seems to be rather like Polo and Gonzo making babies, because the man has to go in here, where the "treasures" are, and later the baby comes out where the man had gone in.' Joy said: 'No, Polo and Gonzo are here; and you are not one of the animal family.' I said: 'Well, perhaps it is like you having secrets which have to be guarded carefully, and you won't let anyone except me in to know about them.' Joy was quite happy with this second comment, but she still wanted to maintain that a drawing is only a drawing. (I had made these comments so that she knew she was allowed to speak about sexual matters, which I could tell – from what I knew about her and from her play – were evidently preoccupying her.)

Reading: After this drawing, any attempts by me to get Joy to concentrate on reading were quite fruitless.

Session 4 (Friday before Christmas)

When Joy began drawing she started with a top hat out of which she made it 'rain upwards'. She said: 'I've drawn that upside down so you won't know what it is.' She made this into a clown. 'But he is really a spy dressed up as a clown, disguised so nobody will recognize him.' I asked her what he was trying to find out: secrets? 'Yes, secrets.' She continued to draw. She made the spy look very unhappy – adding tears to his eyes. At the top of his head she drew a circle and said 'In here he has a little man with a gun, and [still drawing] down here [she drew another circle in his tummy] he has another man with a gun.' 'These are his friends', she said, 'but here comes a flying ball – a ball with teeth.' She drew the teeth in red. She then covered them over: 'so no one will see that it has teeth' and turned the teeth into a broad smile. She further disguised the ball by drawing petals around it, saying: 'It now looks like a flower . . . but here it has a gun' (which she added to one of the petals). She took up the blue felt-pen and drew in the teeth again, and made the eyes blue too.

I asked Joy who were the 'goodies' and who the 'baddies' in her picture. She immediately took this up, saying that the little man inside the spy was 'a goodie' and 'the flying ball with teeth comes from the baddies'. She added: 'I'll be like that and I will have a go at Richard . . . but I haven't got a gun. I'll get a dalek suit for Christmas, and then I'll have a gun and I'll fight Richard.'

Reflection

I saw in this sequence a recurring conflict around Joy showing her aggression and a defensive need to hide it. I also thought that there was a disguised allusion to enuresis in her making it 'rain upwards', drawing rain upside down so that I would not know about it. But, at the same time, she told me that this was what she was doing – to make sure that I did know. The theme of disguise continued with the spy disguised as a clown, and the flying ball with hidden teeth. The petals offered further disguise but there was still a gun which was added to one of the petals – a gun which Richard had, and Joy would like to have.

Monday. Christmas holiday

Session 5 (Tuesday after Christmas)

Joy was difficult and very restless. She wouldn't concentrate so no effective reading work was done. She pulled the table cloth off 'to make everything go on the floor' so I had to remove it. Her only interest was in drawing.

She began with a ground-level line. She drew a little man in a cave and then obliterated him. She drew a dog, crossed it out and turned it into 'an animal with a snakey tail'. She drew what looked like a ladder: 'That is a well, and in the well there is an octopus.' She drew a 'Mummy figure' underneath, a 'Daddy figure' to the right, and 'a boy' to the left. She turned the boy into a girl and drew a hat on his/her head. She drew another black octopus at the top right and a red octopus on the left. She ended by drawing tufts of grass at the bottom. 'This is hair-grass', she said. I made no comment except to say: 'The octopus in the well looks very sad.' She agreed with this. She decided to give him a clown's nose so she drew a cross on the nose. She added a final touch by making the man hold a gun which he was shooting.

Reflection

This was the first session after the break and Joy may still have been over-excited from Christmas. Equally she may have been angry with me for being away. I felt that she might have been telling me that she had felt obliterated by my absence, giving my attention to other people rather than to her, and I noticed that she had obliterated the 'little man' who was by the entrance to the cave. I thought I had been made small in her mind so that she would not miss me.

I felt that the 'sad' octopus might well be herself. By contrast the parent figures were together, outside the well containing the sad octopus, and they had a boy with them (Tom?). She turned this boy into a girl – perhaps placing herself where the boy was.

Session 6 (Wednesday)

Joy was exceedingly difficult. She pushed things off the table and then put her feet on it. She wouldn't even look at the reading material I tried to assemble, and at times she was so frustrating that I felt drawn into becoming a 'punitive parent'. This was clearly a mistake but it also indicated what she was doing to me.

Once I had decided that it was useless to pursue Joy further with the reading material, she began to draw and she became very excited as she did this. In one drawing there were two little men which she called 'chinese mice because they have long tails'. She drew a bird and an aeroplane 'with a bag underneath which it puts round the bird to keep it safe'. And there was another dangling man, hanging from a parachute.

Before the end of this session Joy drew a second picture. 'This is Polo. She is all dressed up for a fancy-dress ball. Mummy and Daddy are going to a ball in fancy-dress. We'll give Polo antlers then no one will recognize her: she will be all disguised. And here are her puppies, and they are disguised too.' I said: 'It looks rather like your Mummy with Richard and Joy – and Tom on her back like a baby that has to be carried.' Joy denied this, saying 'Tom doesn't need to be carried now. He can walk.' She didn't go so far as to deny altogether that this could represent her mother and the three children, but on the whole she still insisted that a picture was 'only a picture' and no more.

Reflection

This session began with an even stronger protest against reading and a wish instead to do drawing. There were further examples of her using disguise.

Session 7 (Thursday)

I was determined not to give in to Joy's attempts to make me angry, but to wait until she decided to join me. She again began by pushing away all reading materials. She wouldn't look at anything I put out for her. She walked round the room ignoring me. But when I continued quietly to put letters out on my own Joy began to be curious. In this way we managed to make a few words that she was prepared to read.

Joy drew her friend Anne, saying that she now thought Anne was silly. She didn't think she wanted to be her friend any more. She put 'A' for her name. She said 'This is you.' I said: 'But isn't this a girl?' 'Yes', she replied, 'but it's still you!' She drew the octopus motif on the skirt, drew a face in the tummy, covered it over with red, drew a circle in the tummy then crossed it out. We looked at the drawing together and I said that it seemed to be a rather angry drawing. She replied with emphasis, 'Now you are right there!'

As I was leaving the room the mother came to see how we had been getting on. Unfortunately, I allowed myself to be persuaded into showing her what progress we had made and I asked Joy to read out our list of words. She did this quickly and confidently, getting the first half right without a pause. When she came to the word 'POT' she hesitated and guessed the rest. She had reverted to her old method of 'reading' by guessing.

Reflection

Joy had begun to show curiosity when I did something on my own rather than thrusting it at her. Her reference to Anne may have been to let me know of her feelings about me. Anne was silly and she didn't want to be Anne's friend any more. (Anne had been associated earlier with reading and wanting to read.) In case I was too silly to get the point Joy made this very explicit by telling me that Anne was me. Joy elaborated on this by using the octopus motif (which she frequently used to represent her mother), and put a baby in the tummy with an 'O' (presumably Oggie – her name for Tom when he had first been born). She had then crossed out the 'O'. I wondered if Joy was beginning to experience me as the mother who didn't spend enough time with her: and what other children or babies did I have that took me away from her when I was not seeing her? She didn't want me to have other babies and crossed out the Oggie baby in her drawing.

Session 8 (Friday)

We started with more three-letter games, as on the previous day, but Joy would not read any of the words that I made. She preferred to continue guessing. She was largely obstructive and refusing to be co-operative.

When she began drawing Joy again drew an octopus. She 'disguised' this by putting trousers round all the legs. She added clown's eyes, a clown's hat and another hat. She drew 'a fish, with teeth, that comes and bites off one of the legs'. Still drawing, she said: 'Now here is a rat with a tail and big teeth. And here is a man with one leg bitten right off. The teeth are red. And here is a hat for the man who has lost his leg, and the fish has a hat. And here is a crab.'

I commented: 'You've drawn a lot of teeth today. Does that mean that you want to bite people because you are angry?' She replied, 'No'. I continued: 'Well, I have noticed that you do draw teeth when you've been angry with me over the reading.' She seemed to accept this but made no actual reply.

Reflection

I had not yet interpreted to Joy the mother transference as I had regarded that kind of interpretation as beyond my 'brief' with her. But she was not deterred. She went straight back to the octopus. She disguised this with trousers. (I was later told by the mother's analyst that the mother 'liked to add to her body image sometimes with hats, sometimes with trousers, and with her phallic behaviour'.)

Joy used clown's eyes as a specific symbol of her own. It could be used to represent me as someone stupid, or to indicate eyes that didn't see, or both. At the time, however, I was still not letting her know if I was seeing what she had been telling me or not. The clown had two hats. I wondered if Joy saw me as 'wearing two hats', one when I was alone with her and another when I was with her mother – as at the end of the previous day's session. This could add to any tendency she may have had to see me as having a split loyalty or as being there really to do mother's bidding.

In her drawing there was a man who had a leg bitten off, and there were also several biting creatures. There was plenty here to suggest castration anxiety but I did not take this up. Instead I focused on the biting. In her response to my comment here Joy showed that I was not getting to the point. I was avoiding the more specific elements in the material. I had also missed the possible allusions to the coming weekend, the days when I would be wearing yet another hat – in my life away from her.

Session 9 (Monday)

A frustrating day. Not much reading got done and her play was listless. I wondered if this could have been her response to the weekend.

Session 10 (Tuesday)

I brought with me (for the first time) a magnetic blackboard with letters. Joy played happily with this but unfortunately her mother came to see me on her way out. I was feeling a bit conscious of having submitted my first account to her and once again fell into giving her some idea of Joy's progress. I told her that we had made about 20 words today. 'Oh good', she replied, 'so Joy will soon be able to start reading the book we have that has only 36 words.'

Reflection

I realized that I would have to resist any premature introduction of reading books into our sessions. Furthermore, I would have to avoid slipping into giving indications of Joy's progress, as this only fed into the mother's anxiety and impatience for tangible evidence of progress. The mother's constant access to me, as I came and went, was also becoming a severe disadvantage.

Session 11 (Wednesday)

Trying to read with Joy was futile. She wanted to put two random letters together and give them names. She resisted all my attempts to get her to make words with me or to read words. This may well have been a reaction to the further contact with her mother the day before.

When Joy began drawing she chose, for the first time, to copy. She copied a painting from the front page of a magazine on a coffee table in the room. The picture was of a 'visitation' scene of some sort, a man approaching a woman sitting under a canopy. Joy made the woman a queen who looked as if she was sitting up in bed. The canopy was used as another version of the octopus motif. There was a king approaching on a horse, sword in hand. Joy added 'a dalek' standing behind the queen. Over the king she put 'an aeroplane with a nose', and above that an octopus with a clown's hat. She made lightning attack the canopy over the

queen, and the octopus fired from one of its legs. Towards
the canopy, and behind the king, there was 'a hidden baddie'
who was 'firing and making it lightning'. At the top she drew the
sun with a little man in it.

I made no comment except to say that there seemed to be a lot
of fighting in the picture. Joy seemed happy drawing this picture,
and I think she liked my comment. I added that she seemed to
like drawing octopuses. She replied: 'But you have to be very
careful with them as they can catch you and can eat you all up, so
that you would then be inside the octopus.

Reflection

We continued to have the octopus motif, here placed clearly in
relation to the mother. There were several implied attacks
against the dangerous octopus-mother, the 'dalek' standing
behind the queen and the 'hidden baddie' behind the king. I
thought that Joy would like to be on her father's side (the
king's), so that she could feel safe there and be able to be
'firing and making it lightning'. I wondered who the little man
in the sun might be. Could this represent me – seen today as
little?

Session 12 (Thursday)

We began with the blackboard which still had the alphabet laid
out on it. While I was laying out the vowels, and two rows of
lower-case letters that could be used with them, Joy made a fresh
exploration into my holdall. There she found a box of magnetic
capital letters. She was delighted with her find and thought her
letters were much better than mine. She immediately put out her
alphabet and laid out three columns of random letters, like in the
spelling game I had been arranging. This was to be *her* game and
she would make the rules! 'You have to close your eyes', she
said, 'to pick your first letter. Then you open your eyes and you
pick two more letters and make up a word. We take turns. . . .
I'll start.'

Joy first picked 'F' and 'H', which she put together. I took this
opportunity to show her that we would have to use one of the five
vowel letters I had put out too. Even in her game we could not
make words without using vowels. I showed her a sequence I had
put out for her – PA, PE, PI, PO, PU – following each with a 'T'
to complete the words. Joy seemed interested when she
discovered that some letters (vowels) are special in this way. We

began playing 'her' game, with vowels accepted into it from 'my' game. The first word she made was her 'favourite word' – NIT. She put this as far away as she could on the board 'so we can't cheat by looking at words we have already made.' The next word she broke up after she had made it, and put it in another corner of the blackboard saying 'I don't like it any more.' I asked if she always pushed things away that she didn't like. She didn't reply.

After this Joy decided that we would write down the words we had made. She took the scribbling pad and roughly ruled a page with a line down the middle. She had a red pen for herself and chose blue for me (the colour that she had used for 'ruling' the lines). She wanted to make a word with AG. I helped her with 'H' and she wrote down HAG on her side. I changed the 'A' to 'U' so she wrote down HUG on my side. She decided it would be better if I chose next. I made the word FUN. She wrote this down on her side as well as mine. She made MEN and again wrote this down on both sides. By now it was the end of the session.

Reflection

For a second time we had been too engrossed to do any drawing. I felt the session had included an important moment because Joy had taken over the spelling game and made it her own. Elements of her controlling me were certainly present too, but she was prepared to accept part of my 'rules' into her game so that vowels were included and real words could be made instead of nonsense combinations. There was a new sense of sharing.

Session 13 (Friday)

When I arrived, Joy was playing with a ball which she had taken from the Christmas tree. This was made from malleable tin foil. She had pushed some dents into this and she showed me proudly how she could make the dents disappear 'by pushing at the corners – on the points', so that she could mend it as well as push it out of shape. She showed me one side of the ball where she had made a lot of holes with a pin. I shook the ball, when she handed it to me, and noticed that there was something rattling inside. I suggested that there was a pin that may have got inside. Joy strongly denied this, insisting that there was nothing at all inside. 'I'll show you', she said. She tried to push a hole in the ball with a pen but it wouldn't go through. She went to look for scissors and said that she would cut it open to show me. I asked her whether she would get into trouble if she cut up the ball. She was sure that nobody would mind, 'and anyway there are plenty more balls on the tree', she added. She made a hole with the point of the scissors. 'That is for you,' she said. 'For me to get inside?' I asked. 'Yes, to find out what is in there.' She made the hole larger. We didn't find anything because whatever it was had fallen on to the floor. She then made it into 'a purse'. 'We can put things into it', she said. I asked 'What shall we put inside?' She continued: 'Money of course, but we haven't got any money so we'll have to make some things to put inside.' She carried on cutting. 'We can make the purse smaller.' By this time it resembled a dish and I commented that the purse was now quite open. 'But we can still shut it up', she replied, 'I'll show you.' She folded it over but it kept springing open again. She then tied it shut 'So that the things inside won't get out.' I asked her if these were secrets. 'Yes', she said. 'And, so that burglars like you won't get in, you are not allowed to know the secrets.' I replied: 'But you can tell me your secrets because you know I won't tell them to anyone else.' (With more experience I would have avoided the use of reassurance here and would have explored her anxiety that she could not yet trust me with her secrets. I should also have recognized that she might experience this as seductive.)

Joy put the purse into her 'pocket'. To do this she had to undo the zip of her skirt. She was ignoring the pocket which I could see on the other side of her skirt as she searched for an imaginary pocket. Joy was trying to hide the 'purse' in her pretend pocket but it wouldn't stay. I suggested that she might use the pocket on the other side (where I could see it). 'No, that pocket has a leak in it, and this pocket has a leak in it too.' She pushed her hand through, to demonstrate this, so that it appeared between her legs – under her skirt. She added: 'You put your hand in here and you'll see that it has a leak.' I answered that I didn't need to do that as she had just shown me. This play ended there and Joy turned to other things.

Reflection

Joy began by playing at damaging the Christmas tree ball, then repairing it. Later she 'destroyed' this and 'created' something else – the purse. She was beginning to explore the question of what is inside things. She made a hole in the ball for me to see what was inside. She made a purse for her 'secrets'. When this wouldn't stay closed she made it smaller. If it was small enough burglars wouldn't be able to get in. I was not allowed to know the secrets today, but then she enacted a seductive invitation for me to look under her skirt at the pocket she has which leaks. (Might this have been her response to my invitation to tell me her secrets? And is she showing me here that she *had* experienced that invitation as seductive? I think so.) What I felt unable to interpret was the richness of her symbolism – her search for the pocket that cannot be seen. Lacking the words to help I focused only on the visible, literal, pocket although she was clearly pressing me to acknowledge the inner 'pocket' that was not being acknowledged by *anybody* – and not yet by me.

Reading: Joy was not interested in spelling games. But, for a time, she was prepared to play 'her' game – making nonsense words. She decided, however, that she would spell POLO because she could do that. She told me that Polo had been away to see somebody who had told them she wouldn't be having babies after all. She was 'half sorry but mostly glad' about this.

I tried to get Joy interested in more spelling but she pushed away the words I was making with the magnetic letters. She walked round the room appearing uninterested, but she soon came to look over my shoulder to see what I was doing. She watched for a while. I was making a few words on my own. She then announced: 'I can spell LOOK, because I know that.' We did this on the board; also BOOK, COOK, and ROOK. I asked her to write down LOOK, which she had correctly spelled out aloud to me. She wrote KOOL. I removed LOOK from the board and suggested that she make it with the letters on the board. This time it was correct. She compared this with what she had written and crossed that out, obliterating it completely, and wrote it again correctly.

Reflection

Having introduced a curiosity about the shape of things, and the 'inside' of things, Joy showed her curiosity with what I was doing. She looked over my shoulder to see and announced that she could spell 'look'. When she wrote this down she reversed it. Here I thought Joy was giving me an indication of her taboo on looking, and her need to reverse what she sees because of the implications for her of seeing things as they are. This may be particularly true in relation to herself and her brothers, who were different from her and were probably treated differently because of this.

Drawing: Joy described what she was doing as she drew: 'I am going to draw the zoo.' She wrote ZOO at the top. She drew a cage. Inside the cage she drew a seal. I said I didn't think seals were put in cages. Joy put in some water. 'They have to be in a cage because, when people come to feed fish to them, if they are not safe inside a cage they might come and water at them – I mean snap at them.' I said I wondered why she had said 'water' just then and she replied that she had meant to say 'Come out of the water and snap at them.' I asked her if she was going to draw someone holding a fish to the seal. She almost shuddered and gave me an emphatic 'NO'. She told me that there was a notice NOT TO FEED THE ANIMALS. 'We'll put it on a notice here', she said, and she wrote 'NOT'. She said: 'That could be for all the things you're not allowed to do.' She decided that it would read NOT TO FEED THE OSTRICHES. She began to draw an ostrich, made it into a seal and called it 'A fat lady resting'. After more thought about her 'NOT' notice she said: 'The notice now says DO NOT DISTURB.' (I gathered later that her mother had been much given to resting and saying that she should not be disturbed, particularly during her pregnancy with Tom.) Joy scrubbed out NOT and drew a spider. She drew a man putting his hand in the cage. 'We'll make him a clown, and here's his clown's hat, and there's his big nose – but it is an artificial nose.'

As I was leaving, Joy said: 'If Mummy asks about the ball I want you to say that you made me cut it open.' She was clearly trying to manipulate me, but she may also have been testing me to see if I would stand up to this. I told her that I couldn't say that because she knew that it wasn't true. She seemed to accept this.

Reflection

The slip of the tongue ('water at') might have referred to Joy's continuing enuresis. There might also be a further allusion to her view of herself as 'castrated' when she shuddered at the thought of someone feeding the snapping seal. In her elaboration around the 'NOT' notice, it was interesting that she saw the prohibitions that she had been subjected to as summed up in the single order not to disturb (the fat lady – a pregnant mother). The 'NOT' notice was replaced by a spider (another archaic symbol for the mother). She followed my earlier lead and drew a man putting his hand into the cage, but he is a clown (stupid?) and his nose was artificial. The 'male' protrusions were either in danger of being bitten off or were artificial (the nose is not really as big as it seems). What might have been there at the very end of the session was a further prompt about Joy's need to be allowed a safe space to play, where if necessary she can cut things up and 'destroy' them without having to be anxious about her mother's reactions. I had not yet managed to tackle this problem.

Session 14 (Monday)

Joy came in carrying some artificial ferns, a long pencil, and some white cloth. With these she played quite contentedly, but after a pause she looked around for something else. She collected an ashtray from the window-seat which contained the ash of one cigarette and one stub-end. 'This is more like it', she said with glee. She obviously enjoyed spilling the ash on to the cloth, scraping it together, digging out the filter tip for more, pulling the ferns to bits and 'planting' these in the ash. After a while she began bombing the ferns with the pencil, saying 'Stinky, smelly, smelly bum; bumble bee; the pencil is a bumble bee.' She was content with this for a bit, but added: 'What we really need now is some water to mix with it.' She wanted to 'slip out' to get some straight away: 'No one will see.' I suggested that it might be rather difficult to use water in the drawing-room. 'Well I'll use it afterwards, but I'll have to do it in secret afterwards so no one will see me. But if I could do it here I wouldn't have to hide it.' I suggested that there were quite a lot of secret things which she would like not to have to hide, and which she could perhaps share with me. She agreed enthusiastically.

Reflection

Joy indicated quite openly her need for greater freedom to play with water and mess. Having been placed so firmly in the drawing-room by the mother, I had not yet found any way to free myself from the mother's control over Joy's 'reading lessons'. The arrangement had therefore remained a compromise between reading and therapy, but Joy could not have made a plainer plea for me to allow her to use her sessions as real play-therapy, without the restriction imposed by the parental setting. She added, sadly, that she would have to do it in secret afterwards, but she wouldn't have to hide this if it were allowed in her sessions.

Reading: Whilst Joy continued playing with the ashtray I began

to put some words out on the blackboard. I tried to encourage
her to come over and join me at the board, but without success.

I turned the board so that she could see it and asked her to
read one of the words there. She turned away. I said: 'Look at it
and tell me what this word is. It's a word that you know.' 'I can't
look because I haven't got any eyes', was her reply. I said that I
thought it was because she didn't want to look that she said she
hadn't got eyes. . . . 'There are some things you don't want
to see.'

Reflection

Joy may have been telling me that I was the one who seemed
to be blind. At that time I failed to see this and interpreted the
blindness as hers, not mine!

As I left, I was again met by the mother who wanted to know
how we were getting on. I took this opportunity to tell her that
I appreciated her wish to see results, but I felt that Joy needed
a time without being expected to perform for her parents.

Comment: Even though I had made a step towards establishing
better boundaries for Joy's sessions I had still not asked for a
more appropriate play-space for our sessions.

Session 15 (Tuesday)

I tried in vain to do reading with Joy but she blocked at every
stage. Instead she made up a game with the magnetic letters,
collecting small 'o's and 'e's. She arranged these with the letters
on their sides (they were oblong in shape) 'so that the 'o's will be
smaller than the 'e's', and she told me that the letters were 'going
to school'. She took a big 'C' and two little 'c's, saying:
'These are the teacher and her two friends who are helping her.'
She built a cage round these with straight letters. 'The 'e's are
the older children, because they are bigger', she explained. 'I saw
Anne yesterday', she said after a pause. I asked if Anne could
read now. 'Yes, easily.' I asked if she is in the class of the 'e's
now, with the bigger children. 'Yes.' (Pause.) 'No, the 'e's are
the smallest children now.' I asked her if she wanted to be able to
read like Anne. 'No, I don't want to read at all.' Joy pushed all
the letters to the sides of the board and said: 'There, I've *never*
seen the board so clear as that!'

At the end of this session I asked Joy why she had wanted to play and not do any reading today. She replied: 'I don't want to read. I want to play.'

Reflection

I still felt under pressure to be the 'reading teacher', and I may still have been wishing to protect myself from entering the unknown area of real play-therapy for which I felt singularly unprepared. Also, I thought that Joy had been giving me further indications of her unease about my contacts with her mother. In fact, in this session Joy seemed to be emphasizing her need for clearer boundaries, by building her wall with straight letters to keep me out, the cage around the big 'C' (for Casement?) and the two little 'c's who were helping the teacher. The need for an adequate play-space was again evident when Joy pushed all the letters to the sides of the board, thus making it clearer than ever before.

Session 16 (Wednesday)[1]

We began by writing. After a while Joy announced that she had forgotten something, and asked to be allowed to go and fetch it. She went out and brought back a torch. 'This is my gun', she announced. She began exploring behind the cushions of the settee, saying 'This is a secret passage.' She climbed into this, burrowing and emerging. I responded to this reference to 'secret passage' and said to her that it was rather like being born. She wasn't too sure about this, but she had so far always rejected such comments from me. (Joy had a rich capacity for phantasy and imagery in her own terms. Interpretations still seemed to be experienced by her as an intrusion into her private world.)

Joy continued playing for most of the session – still burrowing behind the cushions. She turned this into a game. 'I want to see how many cushions I can knock over at one go.' I didn't feel able to offer any interpretation of this, but as these were drawing-room cushions they were clearly parent-related objects that were being knocked about. I felt even more uneasy about this play taking place in such an obviously 'parental' space.

Joy tried fixing the lighted torch under her jumper. 'Look, now no one will know where my torch is', she said. However, as it was still alight it could be seen through her jumper. I thought (to myself) that she was wanting to boast of an obvious penis-like protrusion that I couldn't fail to notice. But, as I didn't know what she called a penis (or if she had any word for it at all), I tried interpreting this more vaguely by saying 'It makes you look like a boy.' She wouldn't accept this. 'What do you mean?' she asked. I replied lamely: 'You know what I mean.'

Reflection

I failed to follow Joy's cue for me to be more direct in speaking of sexual differences. We were not able to put these into words at this stage, because of my continuing reticence about making a specifically sexual interpretation to a child. I did not know whether I could handle whatever might follow from such direct interpretations. (Later events proved that the inhibition here was much more mine than hers.)

Joy probed the lighted torch into everything; into my ear, into my mouth, up her nose. 'Look, I can make it red', she exclaimed. I hesitated to interpret. She told me that she was going to hide under her mother's bed with the torch 'to find out what I can see'. I asked her if her parents slept in the same bed or did they have separate beds. 'The same bed. A big bed. You can see it if you want to.' I asked her if she had ever slept in the same room as her mother and father. 'No, but Mummy sometimes sleeps in my room – when I'm not well.' I said that she probably wondered what her Mummy and Daddy did together in bed. *'No, I don't!'* she replied with great emphasis. I suggested that she had denied this so strongly because she really wanted to know very much. She turned to the settee for a last bit of cushion-bashing. I said: 'Well, I am going now. You can do that when I have gone.' Joy didn't want me to go. She said 'I haven't finished my bashing yet and I can't possibly do that when you have gone. *I can only do this when you are here.*' I said that there were probably a lot of things that she felt she could only do when she was with me. She agreed. She helped me to tidy everything up 'so that it looks all right again', she said.

Reflection

Joy enacted with the torch her wish to look into everything. She needed me to help her understand what she sees (to throw some light on it). She could also have been using the torch to highlight what she is 'saying' in her play, and to demonstrate that she needed me to put this into words for her (the torch into my ear and my mouth). She wanted to show me her parents' double-bed, having indicated that there were secrets there which she needed me to know.

The plea for a play-room was present as ever, and I continued not to act upon it.

Session 17 (Thursday)

Joy wanted to begin by drawing. She drew a house. 'That's *your* house', she said. She drew round windows with a cross over them. I said they looked like clown's eyes. I asked whether the house had clown's eyes so that you couldn't see *out* or couldn't see *in*.' She said 'So you can't see in.' She obliterated the windows, saying 'These are curtains.' She drew a penis-shaped projection out of the side of the house. 'Now, here we have a big sort of thing', she said. I asked her if she had a 'thing' like that. She asked me what I meant, and once again I said 'You know what I mean.' (It was beginning to be almost impossible to stay with euphemisms to describe parts of the body. Names were becoming essential.) 'No', she said, 'I haven't got a thing like that.' She drew animals on 'the thing'. She said, still drawing: 'Here's a great big bird, an eagle – a Condor – with a great big beak and a long tongue, and it's going to come down and attack the animals here. We'll use some red because it is dangerous. Now the bird is coming to get some precious things that you have in your house. You know what?' 'Treasures?' I asked. 'Yes', she replied, 'you keep them in your bedroom there. We'll draw the stairs.' She drew the stairs in red. I asked her if these were in red because it might be dangerous to go up the stairs. 'No, it is not dangerous here because it is in *your* house . . . but it is dangerous where a bird wants to come in. I am going to make a special trap there so that the eagle bird will be caught and you will be safe.' She drew 'a cage thing'. (Pause.) 'Now there are other birds here, and they are dangerous too. They're baddies. But this bird is a good one who has come to look after you to keep you safe from the eagle bird . . . . And here's a cow; no, a bull.' I asked her to show me that it was bull. She drew horns on its head. I asked what it had underneath that made it a bull. She said she had never looked. She continued, 'Now the treasures are hidden in your room. I'll show you . . . .They are hidden behind a picture like this. . . .' She described the picture as she drew it, saying 'It's of a cow; no, a horse.' (I wondered if she had chosen a horse because the sex differentiation is less obvious, and I had questioned her about the bull.) She went on, 'And all round there are secret bomb-things, which will go off if anyone tries to get at the treasures. But they won't go off at you because I will give you the key, which will go in here, and you are the only one who is allowed in.'

Joy drew the detail of the bomb gadgets. She said: 'There are little bombs like these (red spots round the picture) which come out by mistake if you are not careful. . . . And the other big bombs are water-bombs.' I asked which bombs Joy preferred. She replied 'The water-bombs.'

Reflection

Joy pursued the previous day's theme. This time the bedroom secrets were put in my house where they would not be dangerous. The danger was identified as coming from the big eagle bird from which I would need to be protected. She took particular care in drawing the bomb-gadgets around the picture, behind which the secret treasures were hidden. I noted that only I was to have the key to reach these secrets safely. Joy was pressing home the point that her pictures hide (but also show) things, which could be dangerous with other people, but were safe for me to reach with the key. There still seemed to be an unconscious hope that I would interpret these bedroom secrets to her via her pictures.

Reading: I had made a sentence on the magnetic board: IT IS FUN FOR A NUN TO RUN IN THE SUN. As we talked about nuns, Joy said that she knew that they do not marry. She told me that they are not allowed boyfriends because 'If one nun had a boyfriend, the others would want him too, and they might start fighting.' Joy also knew that nuns do not have babies. I noted the implications of the play and the theme of competition for the same man (possibly alluding to Joy competing with her mother for my attention – and for father's) but I did not interpret.

Session 18 (Friday)

Joy played with coal, wanting to smear me with it. She wanted to fetch water to put with the coal so that she could make more mess. She asked me if I could get something so that she could draw on the blackboard. I agreed to get some chalks for next time.

Comment: It was difficult to recall the detail of this session, but the plea for a freer play-space was clearly repeated.

Monday (No session)

Now Christmas was past, the arrangement was that I should see Joy four times a week. This was the first week of the new arrangement.

Session 19 (Tuesday)

Joy started with the white chalks whilst I began writing a few words. Joy began crossing these out with the whole length of the chalk, which she scrubbed up and down making a lot of chalk dust. She went to fetch her mother's box of paper tissues, so that she could wipe the board. This produced more dust, which she started collecting in one corner of the board. She wanted 'to make as much dust as possible. . . .I will throw the dust into your eyes to make them itch so that I can watch you rubbing the itches in your eyes which I have made.' She took a piece of coal, which she wrapped up with one of her mother's tissues, and said: 'This is my baby, a coal-baby, and it is very useful. . . . We can rub out the board and we can rub all the white off.' She experimented putting the coal into her mother's box of tissues, leaving quite a lot of coal dust inside the box. I felt it necessary to shake this out before I left. I was becoming increasingly distressed by Joy's clear need for a different room where she could more easily make mess as part of her play. I decided finally to discuss this with the mother as soon as an opportunity presented itself.

Reflection

The pressures to find a freer play-space had developed to an unmistakable crescendo, and yet I was still avoiding action. But Joy persisted with her own need for something other than the nice polite 'extra reading lessons' envisaged by her mother. With hindsight, I am struck by how strongly I was inhibited by my anxieties about seeing Joy without the constrictions for both of us represented by this parental setting. I had been protecting myself by not acting earlier.

Session 20 (Wednesday)

I didn't take the chalk with me for this session as it had been so distracting last time, and I was not sure how I could contain the use of the chalk without it spreading freely over the drawing-room. (I was now quite alarmed by Joy's determined mess-making, and yet again I had to witness her continued pleading for a more appropriate play-space.)

Joy began by taking more pieces of coal and rubbing the black into my hands. She asked me, just a little anxiously, whether the black would come off again. I reassured her that we could wash it off afterwards.

Attempts at reading were fruitless and I did not press further for this. During the session Joy told me that 'coal-baby' was still all right – she had kept the 'baby' behind the sofa in the drawing-room since the day before. At the end she took me into her parents' bedroom, and through to their bathroom where she watched me washing my hands and 'making everything all right again'.

As I was leaving, I met Joy's mother in the passage. I told her about the need for a real play-room. She said that it would be quite all right for me to see Joy in the children's play-room downstairs, and if we wanted access to water we could use the cloakroom near the front door. (I wasn't all that happy with the cloakroom arrangement, even though it was separate from the adjoining lavatory.) The mother seemed keen to continue talking with me but I felt uneasy about this as I knew Joy always found it difficult to tolerate my contact with her mother. It could mean that her mother might take me away from her, just as her father and her two brothers seemed to have become mother's in some way. I expressed my concern about talking to her without Joy being there too. She took my point, a bit reluctantly I thought, and I left.

Reflection

Joy showed the need for continuity – with the coal-baby that had been hidden in the drawing-room since the day before. She also made it abundantly clear that we were going to need water as well as the freedom to make mess. At least, and at last, arrangements had now been made for us to use the play-room.

Thursday (No session)

Joy's mother had tried to contact me, without success, to say that Joy had become ill suddenly during the night. As I had left before she telephoned I had come as usual. I was let in by the Nanny, who gave me a cup of tea. She explained that Joy had kept her mother up most of the night, having started running a temperature at 11.00 p.m. I wondered to myself if there could have been any connection between this and her feelings about me seeing her mother the day before. I also realized that it might reflect anxieties about the impending change from the comparative safety and parental control of the drawing-room to the play-room which, by comparison, seemed to present no controls at all.

Friday (No session)

I was telephoned at home to be told that Joy was still not well enough for me to see her. Then, because I no longer saw her on Mondays, and I could not change my arrangements to offer a make-up session, it was left that I would see her on Tuesday unless I heard otherwise.

Session 21 (Tuesday)

I was let in by the Nanny who told me that Joy was all right now.

This was our first introduction to the play-room and it was pretty chaotic. Joy was not prepared to attend to anything I said, or to anything remotely connected with reading. She pulled things out of the toy-box and played with these. She climbed around on the swing. She picked things up and hit me with them. She even climbed up on to the back of the chair and jumped on to me several times from behind. I tried to interpret to her what she was doing, saying that she was forcing me to control her. In the end I held her arms to prevent her being actually dangerous to me. When she shouted at me to let her go, I said: 'I will let you go when you are ready to hold yourself.' After testing me once or twice, to see if I meant this, I could feel that she had relaxed in my grip. Then I said: 'I think that you are now ready to hold yourself, but if you are not I will hold you again', and I gradually let go of her. She calmed down immediately.

> Comment: This sequence came to be repeated several times during the time I saw Joy, and it always struck me that she would reward me with some particularly creative play, or work, when I had set limits to her otherwise uncontrolled behaviour. I came to feel sure that this reflected the lack of limits in the home, to which the referring analyst had initially hinted.

When Joy settled down she turned her attention to the seat that she had chosen as hers. She told me straight away that I was not to look behind it, because she had 'secrets hidden there'. She launched into a discussion about mice, saying: 'Mice are funny things, because they have big ears so that when one mouse is putting his nose into another mouse's ear you don't know whether he is feeding the other mouse or whether he is telling it secrets.' At the end of the session Joy took from behind her chair one of her 'secrets', which was something that she could chew. Having chewed this up she made an oblong shape, which she tried to push into one of my ears. I did not interpret this. She made a tiny little plasticine figure, which she said was me, and she put this inside a small plastic purse. I said she had made me into a baby and had put me into this purse, which was 'like a baby bag'. She accepted this without comment. At the very end of the session Joy picked up a toy car, which she tried to put into my mouth. Again I didn't interpret.

While Joy had been making her model in plasticine, I had made a plasticine figure of a man. I made him with a very obvious penis. (I was still trying to delay making a verbal reference to the differences between the sexes, which I felt to be preoccupying Joy.) She said to me, on seeing what I had made: 'He shouldn't have three legs.' I told her that she knew quite well really that it wasn't a third leg, but that it was what her brother Richard has and calls 'a penis'. (I did not know what word, if any, was used in the family for 'penis' but clearly I could not delay any longer my moving beyond non-verbal and euphemistic references to it.) She looked puzzled and didn't seem to like the word. I began to lose courage so I offered her a baby-word saying that if she didn't like the word 'penis' perhaps she might prefer to call it a 'winkle', adding that some people called it that instead. She laughed to herself, saying: 'Winkle, twinkle, little star; how I wonder what you are!' and she pulled the penis off the figure. She later pulled various bits of plasticine apart and threw them about the room. She was making a great joke of it – laughing at the word 'penis', at the penis itself, and at me.

Reflection

I thought that it was extraordinary how explicitly Joy had been illustrating her need for me to interpret her sexual curiosity and anxieties about it. She had put into my ear one of the chewed up secrets, which she had produced from behind her chair, as an acted-out version of what she had described earlier as going on with the mouse (his nose in another mouse's ear) which I had failed to take up at the time. It seemed that Joy was indicating that the absence of words for the vital questions and areas of anxiety was becoming an urgent matter for her as well as for me. She was almost forcing into my mouth the words for her secrets that she had so often pointed to.

At the end of the session I was feeling depressed by the amount of mess and 'destruction' that seemed to have come out in the session. (I was also wondering whether it had really been all right to have been so direct with her.) But Joy then surprised me (as I was about to leave) by announcing: 'Tomorrow we will do writing.' She seemed to be saying 'Thank you' for this very different session.

Session 22 (Thursday)

Joy started with writing but this soon turned into play. She drew a large snake. Now, feeling somewhat encouraged by Joy's response to yesterday's session, I said quite directly that this was a penis and she replied with delight: 'Yes, a great big dangerous penis.' She drew two baby snakes beside the big one. I said perhaps these were Richard and Tom. She took the pen that she was using and began poking it into a hole she had made in some paper. I told her that she was pushing a penis into a baby-hole, because a part of her would like to have a penis like Richard and Tom. She accepted this and extended the idea to the wish to have a water-pistol. Richard used to have one and she loved shooting water at people and playing with his pistol. 'I know what you would call it', she said, 'you would call it a star.' I told her that she had called it a 'star' because the previous day I had suggested that she could call the penis a winkle, and she had then said 'Winkle, twinkle, little star. . .'. She continued to play around this theme. At one point she began pushing a pencil in and out of my hair, saying that she was washing my hair. I asked her what she was washing my hair with, was it with a water-pistol? 'No, it is a penis . . . . A great big penis.'

In the course of this play Joy made a plasticine 'Daddy' and gave him a huge and unmistakable penis. She also made a 'fat Mummy'. She was happy with my comment that the Mummy was fat because the Daddy had given her a baby with his big penis. I added 'One of your most precious secrets is that inside your own body you have what Mummies have, which one day (when you are grown up) will make it possible for you too to make a baby inside you.' She smiled happily at me and announced: 'Tomorrow we will read.'

Reflection

I had at last begun to speak directly to Joy about the parts of the body, and she had responded with an equal directness. But, as if to check that she was really allowed to be direct, Joy half teased me by saying that she knew what I would call a penis: I would call it 'a star'. She may also have been reminding me what was echoing in herself 'How I wonder what you are!' – referring to the penis. (There is of course an even more important question around here in Joy's wondering about her own sexual identity, particularly in the light of the preference given to boys in her family.) Joy then showed me that she is wondering about poking a penis into holes. I took this up and put it into words for her. She continued the session by playing at giving me a baby (washing my hair 'with a great big penis') and she played at 'Mummies and Daddies' with the plasticine.

Session 23 (Friday)

Joy seemed to be very much in control of the situation from the moment I arrived. There were some children playing outside the french window 'having a tea party'. Joy came in from the garden, closed the window, and made it quite clear to these other children that if they didn't go away she would draw the blinds down on them. She also waited until the Nanny had gone out of the room before settling down.

Joy wanted to start the session straight away with the blackboard. First she put out the capital letters. While she was sorting out the little letters, she hesitated over the difference between the little 'h' and the little 'n'. I told her that the 'h' had a tail but the 'n' had had most of its tail cut off. She looked at me mischievously and said she knew what I meant: 'The 'n' had had its penis cut off . . . cut off by a big snake.' She added: 'But not a man snake . . . a lady snake.' Having finished with the letters, she asked me if I had remembered to bring some reading books.

We looked at the two books that I had and she chose the easier one. She read this without help from me except for the words 'at' and 'to'. Apart from these words she read the whole book unaided. (This was the first time that she had ever read anything except isolated words.) She had got within a few pages of the end when the time came for the end of the session. I told her that we could leave the rest of it until next time, but she asked if she could have extra time. I replied that she could have ten minutes more if her mother said she could, so she ran outside to ask. When she returned she finished the book in no time at all.

We still had some time left and Joy began playing with Richard's airgun. I told her that she was playing at having a penis. She accepted this and produced a box of beads. She began playing with these, putting them down the barrel of the airgun. I said that she was loading a penis with baby-seeds, and I added that I could use the airgun and the beads to show her how babies are made.

I took a teddy bear and 'hid' this inside my holdall which I had continued to bring to each session. (This still contained all 'her' things.) We put more 'baby seeds' into the gun and we poked the gun into the bag. I said to her 'We are now putting the baby seeds into the Mummy.' She immediately added: 'And then the Mummy becomes all fat and then the baby comes out from inside the Mummy.' After a pause she said: 'I think the baby is ready to come out now.' I produced the teddy bear from inside the bag and gave it to her. She looked radiant.

After this I cleared up my things and Joy went into the kitchen to have her tea. However, as I was turning my car outside the house, she came out of the front door and made sure that she caught my eye to wave 'good-bye'.

Reflection

I felt that Joy and I had shared an important experience, which we would be able to build on in the future. I had at last begun to respond to her cues openly and directly, and there was a great sense of relief (for me as well as for her) from my having been able to put sexual issues into words. It seemed to follow that this 'allowed' Joy to begin to attend to written words, to look at them, to recognize them, to say them aloud and in fact to reveal to me the extent to which she had already begun to learn how to read. In parallel with this I had let myself 'read' what I had written in my own notes, and I had let myself 'see' and to begin to understand the implications of this for Joy.

What also seemed now to have become clear was that Joy had developed a resistance to looking. Although she could clearly see the sexual differences between herself and her brothers, nobody had helped her to understand these differences except in terms of some lack in herself. It had therefore become far more pressing for her to be helped to understand the hidden things about herself as a girl, for which she needed me to provide the words, than for her to be expected to understand those other words that her parents so much wanted her to be learning. Reading followed naturally after her own more urgent needs here were beginning to be attended to.

Follow-up

My detailed notes on this work with Joy ended with the last session given here, but the therapy went on. It was not the end of her problems but the beginning of a more direct way of dealing with them.

I continued to see Joy for another fifteen months. During this time her reading was handed back to the school and the parents, with whom it seemed more properly to belong, whilst I continued to offer a setting in which Joy could regress when she needed to. She moved up at school from 'kindergarten' to 'remove', but said that she liked seeing me 'because with you I can be kindergarten, when I feel that's what I want, and you don't mind that.' She also began to discover that her capacity to read could bring attention just as her refusal to read had previously.

A lot of movement occurred in Joy's therapy around the birth of a daughter in my family. I eventually decided to mention this impending event to her because I had always been reliably there for her sessons, but now I might have to miss seeing her on the day of the birth. So I told Joy that my wife was expecting a baby and that it would be born fairly soon. However, I promised that I would telephone if I could not be there for her on the day.

Joy was able to work through her anxiety about this information during the remainder of the pregnancy and she was in the end able to accept, as a good event, the arrival of this baby as it did not take me away from her (as had happened with her mother after Tom's birth). In her phantasy, the baby became 'her' baby and in her play she explored having the baby inside her, giving birth, feeding and looking after it. This helped to reinforce a positive value in her being a girl, and she began to enjoy the fact that women can do important things that men can't do. She was also pleased that I was so clearly delighted at having a daughter.

As Joy began to discover her growing ability in reading, my role of 'reading teacher' became redundant. Her investment in my therapeutic role, however, remained.

The most crucial need that Joy continued to present was for help with her view of herself as a girl, not only different from her two brothers and her father but also so glaringly different in her mother's attitude to her. And it had been a female snake, not a male snake, that she spoke of as cutting off a penis (see session 23).

Having felt so much less valued than her brothers, as though something might be missing in her, we can readily appreciate Joy's excitement and delight upon discovering that her femininity contained hidden mysteries ('secrets') which could give her a positive female identity. She had needed a relationship in which her sexuality could be both acknowledged and contained, and I believe that it helped that she was seeing a male therapist.

Joy's bed-wetting also showed a great improvement and finally disappeared altogether. She had decided to take over the management of this, with the help of an alarm clock (her own idea), and began getting herself up in the night. As with her reading, she discovered a pride in her own achievements.

Discussion

I feel that there is much to be learned from this case. If Joy had been referred to a qualified therapist, she would presumably have been seen in a consulting-room away from her home; the mother would have been much less able to impose her presence upon the therapeutic relationship; there would have been facilities immediately to hand for Joy to use, including water and sand or other means of making mess; there would have been a play-space that allowed for greater freedom than the parents' drawing-room did; and the therapist would have been trained to recognize, and to act more promptly upon, the need for more direct interpretation. The therapy would, therefore, have started better and would have proceeded along expected classical lines.

Instead, we have an opportunity here to witness a child repeatedly giving active cues for me to respond to her most pressing needs. And, by following these leads (as I gradually developed the courage to respond to them), I eventually began to grapple with those key issues.

The naivety of this untrained approach highlights what Joy needed from a therapeutic relationship. Persistently, and with increasing clarity, the process of her unconscious search showed me where she needed to go. I had to learn to follow.

Chapter four

Countertransference and interpretation[1]

What the analyst feels in the session may convey important diagnostic clues for understanding elusive communications from the patient. Ways have then to be found to make use of such clues. A detailed clinical example is given to illustrate some of the problems of interpreting from the countertransference and the therapeutic benefits that can emerge.

In this chapter I present a case that will illustrate more fully some of the concepts outlined in Chapter 1, in particular those of role-responsiveness and projective identification as forms of unconscious communication. I shall give a detailed account of my work with a patient with whom these issues turned out to be crucial; and I will share with the reader some of my internal supervision, as I tried to distinguish what belonged to me (in what I was feeling) from what my responses to the patient might be indicating about her.

It is, of course, essential that we do not interpret just on the basis of what we are feeling. This is all the more important because some patients will actually welcome it, when it gratifies their passivity and their wish to be drawn into a state of merging with an analyst who appears to be all-knowing. Other patients, however, will experience it as omnipotent, intrusive, and persecutory.

A further problem with this patient was that of finding ways in which I could validly draw upon what I was feeling, without having her experience my interpretations as a repetition of her traumatic experiences. To that end I relied upon two safeguards in particular. First, I knew that I had to take note of my own warning to others:

Any . . . interpretation that is based upon interactive

communication needs to be linked to some identifiable cues from the patient, that he or she can recognize when made aware of them. When we cannot identify these cues, this usually indicates that there are not yet sufficient grounds for an interpretation if it is arrived at solely through the therapist's responses to the patient.

(Casement 1985: 99)

Second, I made regular use of trial identification with the patient before attempting to interpret. (I examine the issue of trial identification and interpretation in more detail in Chapter 9.)[2]

Clinical example

The patient (Miss A) was thirty-five when she came to me for help with a severe agitated depression that had a very long history. At the time of the first sequence that I shall describe she had not yet committed herself to analysis. I was then seeing her twice a week. By the time of the second sequence she had been in five-times-a-week analysis for about a year. The analysis continued for three years after that.

Miss A came to England in her early thirties, having lived her life until then in Scotland; the second child of rigid Presbyterian parents, she has an older brother and two younger sisters.

At the age of seventeen Miss A was seriously injured after being knocked off her bicycle by a lorry. She was thought to have sustained some brain damage but the extent of this had never been clear. For most of the next ten years she had been in hospital.

About six months after the accident Miss A had begun to develop agitated movement of her arms and legs. This soon became so severe that she could no longer walk. The cause of this agitation was assumed to be the supposed brain damage. Very soon she became confined to a wheel-chair, and within months she had also become doubly incontinent. Because of this her hospital management was relegated to a geriatric ward. There, still a teenager, she was shut away with elderly deteriorating patients; and there she remained until she was discharged ten years later.

While she was in hospital Miss A had been treated by a psychiatrist who had persistently used a treatment method that he called 'catharsis'. (Although not psychoanalytically trained he had apparently called himself a psychoanalyst, and this made for considerable problems in the patient's transference to me when I later took her into analysis.) That cathartic treatment involved urging the patient to recall details of the accident using suggestion, hypnosis, and various 'truth' drugs. After some of these sessions the attendant nurse was called to witness that Miss A had shown 'unmistakable pelvic movements' whilst unconscious. This was meant to prove the sexual origin of her conversion symptoms.

Ten years later, the agitation in the patient's legs was sufficiently controlled for her to recover her ability to walk. This recovery resulted from an experimentally intense course of ECT. She did not, however, lose the agitated movements of her arms, which meant that she still had to control the shaking of one hand by holding it in the other. This had been her condition until she came to me.

For much of the first year of my seeing Miss A, she would come to each session in a ritualistic way. The ritual included defecating before many of her sessions, and quite often again afterwards; and in each session, as if by contrast, she talked in a lifeless and boring way of the daily details of her many years in hospital.

My capacity for sustaining a spontaneous interest in this monotonous outpouring began to be sorely tried. I would find myself switching off, sometimes almost entirely. How then was I to go on seeing this patient who was beginning to bore me out of my mind? This became a crucial issue, requiring active and thorough self-examination.

I struggled with my unruly feelings towards this patient in every way I knew. Was this just personal countertransference? Did Miss A represent some other relationship for me, from which I might be retreating into boredom as a defence? But I could not recognize anything that really confirmed this. Or was it simply that I did not like the patient? Had Winnicott been pointing to something like this in his paper 'Hate in the countertransference'? (Winnicott 1958: ch. 15). Perhaps I just couldn't stand her! And yet I felt a real concern for her – and basically I liked her. I therefore did not think that I had yet understood this response that was troubling me.

Gradually, however, I began to notice a striking similarity between how I was feeling towards this patient and how she described her father being with her. He had visited her in hospital, regularly twice a week, but he had merely listened to her complaints about the treatment of her. He never did anything to have this changed. It was as if he either did not care, or perhaps he could not cope with seeing his daughter in a geriatric ward – unable to walk and doubly incontinent. Perhaps he just switched off from the appalling facts of her life. (The mother was even more absent, having felt unable to see her daughter in hospital.)

I wondered how Miss A might have related to this switched-off father. Perhaps she had retreated into a hopeless non-relating, telling the details of day-to-day life in the hospital as a substitute for real relating. I then began to feel convinced that this was what she was doing with me. She was relating events to me; she was not really relating to me with anything of herself. She was also not expecting me to be emotionally engaged by her, or interested in her. In effect, therefore, I had virtually become an embodiment of the switched-off father. I now saw this as a clear example of unconscious role-responsiveness, the patient's contribution to this being her *non-relating* to me in her sessions.

My next problem was to know how to use this insight interpretively. By monitoring each possible interpretation, through trial-identifying with the patient, I discounted the idea of making any direct reference to my feeling bored. It was easy to see that Miss A would immediately have become defensive, feeling criticized, if I made any reference to this before I had found a clear context within which we might be able to look at this phenomenon together.

However, I soon realized that I could approach this from another angle. I could explore with her the way in which she was relating to me. It was then quite easy for me to say to her: 'I am feeling puzzled about something. . . . I have noticed, for some time now, that you frequently speak to me as if you are not expecting me to be interested in what you are saying.'

The patient remained silent. After a pause, I continued: 'It has occurred to me that you may be relating here as you did to your father – at the time when he used to visit you in hospital. You became used to him not doing anything about what was happening to you. I think that you are also expecting me not to do anything with what you are telling *me*.'

The patient then came out of her silence and remarked upon other similarities between her father at that time and how she was experiencing me now. For instance, she also noticed that I was seeing her for an hour twice a week – just as her father had at visiting time.

After this confrontation the patient began to relate to me more as a person, and there were occasional glimpses of some kind of emotional relationship to me beginning to develop. I stopped feeling bored, and the patient became more committed to analytic treatment. Soon afterwards she asked me to take her into analysis; and, when I could, I began to see her five times a week.

During the first year of full analysis the patient continued to use her sessions to pour out details of her resentment to all those who had failed to help her in the past; and I was silently wondering how I too might be failing her in the present. Sometimes I would try to explore this with her but with little result. For much of the time the patient would revert to using me as a passive container for all that she was trying to get rid of in herself.

I was also aware of the patient's continued use of the toilet, before and after her sessions, which prompted me to think that she was using this to re-enact what she had been doing in her sessions with me. Perhaps I was still a 'toilet-analyst' into whom she was seeking to evacuate all that she wished to be relieved of.

However, the way in which I next found myself being disturbed by this patient took a more difficult and worrying form. I found myself quite regularly becoming aware of a slight sexual arousal in myself during her sessions; and this happened only with this particular patient. What was this about? I had to wonder whether I was in some way experiencing the patient transferentially, and responding to her as a sexual object: had my earlier boredom been a defence against this sexual arousal?

I was unable to find any confirmation of this. I could not sense within myself any sexual interest in this patient; nor did she remind me of anyone from whom I might be transferring a sexual significance to her. Nor was I convinced by an alternative supposition, that this sexual arousal was an avoidance of my previous boredom.

I began to wonder whether I was picking up some unconscious communication from the patient. Could my response to her be evidence of some projective identification? But, even if this were so, there was no obvious link between what she was saying and what I found myself feeling. What she was talking about was never in the slightest way related to sexual matters. Could it be that I was feeling what the patient was not allowing herself to feel?

I reviewed what I knew about the patient in this light. Then certain details of her history began to come back to me, and they could now be seen in a new way. For instance, I had heard so many details about her accident, and its aftermath, I had almost forgotten that the patient had not remained continuously in hospital from the time of the accident. She had actually recovered enough to return to work after only three months; and she had been back at work for a further three months before the agitated movements had led to her being re-admitted to hospital. I then began to recall what precipitated her return to hospital. This had been an experience on holiday. She had met a man who had started petting her and then kissing her. She had never been kissed before; she was therefore very surprised when the man put his tongue into her mouth. She was disgusted by this and withdrew, feeling shocked.

When the patient got home from holiday she told her mother about this, wanting to know whether it was how people usually kiss – or was there something the matter with this man? Her mother had not helped with her anxiety or her curiosity. She had simply said 'May God forgive you' (as if she herself could not) and had walked away from her daughter in disgust.

The patient had felt very let down by this dismissive response. She remembered feeling upset that her mother did not seem to see there was something about the experience which she needed to talk about. That same day she had found herself shaking all over. By the next day her shaking had become so bad that her parents had taken her to the hospital for investigation. Within the next two days she had become incapacitated to the point of no longer being able to stand or to walk. Her withdrawal from the world of sexuality became virtually complete when she sub-sequently found herself in a wheel-chair, and later admitted to a geriatric ward.

A lot of things now began to make a new kind of sense. The patient had regressed from genital sexuality to anality; and she had been using the toilet for the evacuation of her anal excitement, as something still to be got rid of as disgusting. I now began to sense that she had also begun to use her relationship with me to get rid of her still disowned genital arousal – into me.

The technical problem was, once again, to see how to interpret from this unconscious level of communication. If I were to interpret too directly from my own feelings I would be behaving seductively. In effect I would be allowing myself to enact towards the patient a near-repetition of how the man on holiday had behaved towards her. Trial identification with the patient was essential here to clarify the technical issue of how *not* to interpret.

It now began to dawn on me that I had been missing an obvious clue. The patient was telling me about everything *except* about what she was feeling. And, in particular, she always spoke of herself as if she were entirely asexual.

I thus felt able to say to the patient: 'One thing stands out, in what you have been telling me since you first came to me. You never speak of yourself as having any sexual awareness: at least, I have heard of only one exception to this – the kissing on holiday.' Miss A replied: 'I never have any sexual feelings. I am probably afraid of them. In fact, it might be more true to say that I am terrified of feeling sexual, and I can't think why.'

The patient told me more about the sequence which led up to her return to hospital. The kissing incident, mentioned by her in passing at her initial consultation, was clearly central. For some reason the patient had become terrified. It was not just that she had felt disgusted by having a man's tongue in her mouth. There was something about her own feelings that had upset her.

The patient now began to realize that she had been excited by this sexual attention from a man, but she had feared that something terrible might follow from it. She at first thought that this might have been due to a fear of becoming pregnant. I therefore explored with her the effects of childhood phantasies, such as that of oral impregnation, as they might relate to this experience of sexual contact with a man. But something continued to be missing. Why should the patient have been so terrified?

At some stage the patient was telling me again how extremely upset she had been about the kissing incident on holiday. She added that she 'could have died with shame' when her mother called upon God to forgive her. I found myself silently wondering about this casual remark. This phrase is a common one, but the patient may have been using the issue of shame to cover something else. The patient was linking her experience of feeling sexually aroused with the thought that she 'could have died'.

I returned to what I knew about the patient. In reality, she had very nearly died when she had been knocked off her bicycle. There was also another detail she had repeatedly included in her narrative of that event. She had always linked the accident with the fact that it happened on the very first occasion when she had ridden a bicycle with drop handlebars. She had asked her brother to turn the handles of her bicycle upside down to make it more like his.

We had previously explored this in terms of her wish to be like her brother. She had also tried to explain the accident in terms of her not having seen the lorry in time to swerve. She thought this had been because she was not used to having her head down rather than sitting more nearly upright as before.

I then started thinking again about my puzzling experience of sexual arousal, which I now felt sure was unconsciously being stirred in me through the patient's powerful disowning of this in herself. Had I been missing an element of sexual arousal in the patient at the time of the accident?

By this time I had been able to show the patient how she had been trying to eliminate from her life anything even remotely connected to her own sexual feelings: her not speaking of anything sexual in her sessions, the absence of any sexual interest throughout her life since the accident, and the use of the toilet as a way of trying to eliminate (outside of the consulting-room) any excitement that might be stirring in her.

Once again, using trial identification, I monitored what I thought of saying. If I were to be too direct with my hunch about her disowned sexuality, I would be putting ideas into her head and she could feel intruded upon. If I approached this too obliquely she could experience me as afraid of her sexuality.

I therefore said to her that we may have been missing something important about the accident. She had discovered that she felt terrified of feeling sexual, and she had responded to the kiss as to something terrifying. Could it be that she had come to see sexual feelings as in some way linked to her experience of a near-death?

What then gradually emerged, from this fresh wondering about the accident, was a recovery by the patient of a severely repressed memory. She recalled having discovered a quite new sensation from riding her cycle with the handlebars dropped. This position had brought her clitoris into contact with the saddle of her cycle. It then became apparent that, at the moment of her accident, she had been carried away by the discovery of a masturbatory excitement in this altered way of cycling. She had therefore experienced the accident as a terrifying result of having allowed herself to experience sexual stimulation. This had also established an unconscious link between sexuality and punishment, with near-death as a dreadful embodiment of that punishment.

The kiss now made sense in an entirely new way. The patient had not immediately associated this re-experiencing of sexual arousal with that earlier (but still repressed) experience. But, when her mother had responded punitively with her dismissive and critical remark, the unconscious link between sexual arousal and near-death was once again imminent. Her agitation since then had continued to express this associative link whilst also defending her from the risk of any further sexual encounter.

The patient was now able to tolerate having the 'unmentionable' mentioned in her sessions. Much working through of this new insight was necessary and, of course, had to be worked through also in the transference.

One day, several months later, the patient reported that she had noticed something quite new. She no longer had to hold one hand in the other to stop it shaking. In fact the agitated movements had almost entirely stopped. This was after twenty years of constant agitation.

Discussion

As well as the physical trauma that led to this patient being admitted to hospital, she had been further traumatized by her treatment there. As described by Miss A, this treatment appears to have been very invasive and was experienced as psychological rape. It was therefore not surprising that Miss A had retreated behind her symptoms and her narrative, defending herself from any further closeness to a man.

By means of my unconscious role-responsiveness, during the early months of her treatment with me, I was able to get in touch with her fear of relating. Only then could Miss A begin to engage with me in the analytic process.

The significance of what later emerged, when I sensed that Miss A was ridding herself of her sexuality, can be better understood if we bear in mind that earlier treatment. From the patient's point of view, her psychiatrist had been seen as trying to force something sexual upon her – and even more persistently than the man who had kissed her. It was clear to me that this patient could not have tolerated any further interpretation of her repressed sexuality until she was ready for this. I therefore decided to wait.

I had little idea of how I would know when this patient was ready for sexual interpretation. Perhaps she would begin to have dreams with recognizable sexual content; or, maybe, she would begin to introduce her own more direct allusions to sexuality into her sessions. Neither of these things happened. Instead, however, I began to realize that the patient's disowned sexuality was beginning to be actively present in the session – *but not in her*. I was therefore able to arrive at the possibility of interpreting this to Miss A with a timing that was specific to where she was in relation to her sexuality. This was now dynamically evident within the analytic relationship, whereas in the earlier treatment it had still been fiercely repressed.

I hope I have been able to illustrate the value of interpretations that arise from monitoring what the analyst is feeling in the presence of the patient. In addition, I have wanted to outline some of the silent dialogue within the analyst that constitutes internal supervision. We can often avoid giving premature interpretation by examining, from the patient's point of view, what we might say – before speaking.

Monitoring what I was feeling in the presence of this patient helped to alert me to what I might otherwise have missed. Later, by using trial identification with the patient, I became able to find ways of exploring the patient's contribution to what I was feeling, without traumatizing her by saying more directly how I got to my understanding. I believe that it was through working in this way that progress was achieved in this analysis that might otherwise have remained impossible. And when, eventually, I did formulate interpretations that were based upon my countertransference these were more than just an application of theory. In each case the impact on the patient was that of real discovery.[3]

Chapter five

The experience of trauma
in the transference[1]

It often happens that past trauma comes to be re-experienced within the analytic relationship. But for this to be effectively worked through, the patient needs to be able to recover an awareness of the difference between the objective present and the past that is spilling into the present. Sometimes the transference experience can be so like the past as to become in itself traumatic. Illustrations are given to highlight the implications for the patient of either too much incidental similarity in the transference relationship, or deliberate difference, as presented by the analyst.

Some terms defined

In *The Language of Psychoanalysis*, Laplanche and Pontalis describe *psychical trauma* as: 'An event in the subject's life defined by its intensity, by the subject's incapacity to respond adequately to it, and by the upheaval and long-lasting effects that it brings about in the psychical organization' (1973: 465). However, not every experience of trauma is a specific event: it can be cumulative (Khan 1974: ch. 3). *Silent trauma* (Hoffer 1952) refers to the effects of cumulative stress, whether in childhood or in the course of analytic therapy. This is often difficult to deal with as the causes are less clear than with more specific trauma.

In this chapter I also wish to emphasize the double nature of *transference*, and the overlap in this between past and present (see Casement 1985: 6–8). Klauber also says something similar: 'The transference illusion is not simply a false perception or a false belief, but the manifestation of the similarity of the subjective experience aroused by an event in the past and in the present' (Klauber *et al.* 1987: 7).

The patient's experience of the analytic relationship is certainly not all transference. There are often elements of objective reality

75

that function as triggers for transference (Gill 1982; Langs 1978). This is part of what I understand Klauber to be referring to when he speaks of the need for 'horizontal analysis' (of what is happening in the here and now) alongside 'vertical analysis' (the historical approach to transference). And he says of this horizontal dimension in the analytic relationship: 'What had been experienced in the past was also being enacted in a relationship between two persons in the present' (Klauber *et al.* 1987: 26). This enactment in some measure involves the analyst as well as the patient.

Central to my argument in this chapter is the concept of *signal anxiety*. In defining this, Laplanche and Pontalis write: 'The signal of anxiety is a reproduction in attenuated form of the anxiety-reaction originally experienced in a traumatic situation: it makes it possible for defensive operations to be set in motion' (1973: 422). Related to this, I believe it is also helpful, when considering the re-experiencing of trauma, to think in terms of *unconscious sets* (Matte Blanco 1975). This gives us a logic in terms of which we can understand how the mind unconsciously registers particular elements of traumatic experience as belonging together – because they have previously been specifically experienced together. They thus come to be established as linked, timelessly and without exception. Matte Blanco also shows us that (to the unconscious) *the part can represent the whole* and that *past, present, and future are all the same.*[2] The result is that anything associated with a trauma can come to represent the trauma as a whole and may trigger signal anxiety, alerting the unconscious mind as if that trauma were about to be repeated. And if several things associated with a trauma again happen to occur together, there is a heightened sense of that trauma again being about to happen.

In order to embody these concepts, I shall give two clinical vignettes. In the first example we can see signal anxiety occurring in response to a set of associations that may still have been conscious.

Unconscious sets in the making

Example 5.1

A baby girl of one year was taken by her mother for inoculation, prior to going abroad. Before injecting the baby's thigh, the doctor asked the mother to pull up her baby's dress.

Up to this point nothing unfamiliar was happening, except perhaps for the presence of this comparative stranger – the family doctor. However, after being shocked by the sudden pain of the injection, it was some months before this child was able to recover from the experience. It seemed to be for ever imminent. Most specifically, she demonstrated clear signal anxiety whenever her mother tried to change her clothes.

Any attempts by the mother to pull up the child's dress were reacted to by screaming. A similar response was evident upon removing other garments; the nearer to the lower half of her body the more intense was the reaction. Other people were trusted with more undressing of the child than the mother, but nobody was allowed to pull up her dress.

We can see in this example how various associations relating to the danger situation had been established around the original trauma. The most specific were the following: *the mother holding her baby on her lap* and *pulling up the dress*. Lesser associations could be identified too: *clothes near to the thigh* and *people like the mother*. It was noticeable that the father was trusted more than the mother, when the child was on his lap instead of hers. But when the child was on someone else's lap, the father became a source of anxiety if he then held out hands to help with any undressing.

Therefore, it would seem, there were different levels of association operating: a lap-person who was a woman being feared more than a lap-person who was a man, particularly if associated with trying to remove clothing. Also, a man holding out hands to help, if associated with trying to remove clothing, was feared more than a woman holding out hands to help.

In this example we can see that the trauma came to be associated with a set of principal elements: *being on a woman's lap*; *clothes being removed or lifted*; *a man holding out hands to do something.*

The mother, intuitively recognizing the associations to which her child was responding, found a way of dealing with this problem. She created differences by putting the child into a bath rather than try to undress her on her lap. She was then able to remove clothes that were wet rather than dry. Wet clothes had not been any part of the original trauma, so this difference enabled the child to accept a new way of being undressed even though *removing clothes* was still part of what the mother was doing. She was, therefore, not completely avoiding the feared experience but finding a way of facing it – as much of it as the child was yet able to tolerate. Gradually, the associative links became weaker and dry clothes could be removed too: first, if removed when sitting in an empty bath, and eventually whilst sitting on mother's lap.

Unconscious sets in the transference

In my second example we can see evidence of signal anxiety in response to a set of associations that was more clearly unconscious.

Example 5.2

A male patient aged twenty-five sometimes experienced acute anxiety between sessions and over weekends. He sometimes had the phantasy that I had become ill or had died. If the telephone rang at such a time as this, he became afraid to answer it – as if this were bringing confirmation of his phantasy. What was happening in the transference?

It emerged that in his early teens this patient had begun to face his father with difficult feelings he had never previously shown so directly to him. During these confrontations he had begun to communicate much that had earlier seemed entirely taboo. For example, he had expressed extreme resentment at the emotional distance that had existed between them for all the remembered years prior to this, and anger at his father for preferring his younger sister.

In the course of several weeks with his father there were crucial changes taking place in their relationship. Most particularly, *the son was expressing difficult feelings* and *he was being listened to*. Previously he had imagined that he could never dare to confront his father in this way: 'It would have killed him.'

The son was now discovering, to his surprise, that it was actually safe to be this direct with his father. What was more, he discovered that he could also love his father as well as hate him. Then, one day when the patient was at school, the news was *telephoned* through to say that his father had suffered a pulmonary embolism and had died.

What had been happening in the transference could be better understood once we had identified some of the unconscious links to a past set of experiences. There were several similarities between the time before the father's death and what was happening in the patient's analysis: he was talking with a man whom he sometimes experienced as his father; in the transference he was confronting the analyst with his anger and his criticism; he was being listened to. These experiences were then followed by an absence – the analyst not being there. Because there had been a similar set of experiences associated with the father's death, absence at a critical time had come to be unconsciously equated with death. The telephone was therefore being feared as the means by which news of this death would reach the patient.

In the transference illusion, I had become (between sessions) the dead father. The patient's distress at his father's death, being re-experienced in these ways, could then be brought to sessions where I (who had not died) could help the patient with his feelings about my 'death' (his father's death) during these times of absence. His mother, too distressed herself at the time, had not been able to help him in this way. For years, therefore, the patient had felt that only his father would have been able to understand how impossible his death had been for the patient to bear. But his father, being dead, could not be there to help him. So, it seemed as if no one would ever be able to understand, or to help him with, the effects of his father's death upon him – and the timing of it.

Doubleness in the transference

We can see in this example a theme which runs throughout this chapter – that of the double nature of the transference. Clinical findings show that a patient needs to discover enough that is different in the analytic relationship to represent security, for it then to be possible for the patient to tolerate the re-experiencing of trauma in the transference. Elements of similarity in the analytic situation can then be used to represent traumatic experience as it was. Both dimensions are necessary, the similarity as well as the difference, for the analytic experience to be therapeutic.

Therefore, if the analyst is obtrusively different (from whichever key person in the patient's life), the patient is deflected from using the analyst in the transference to represent that particular object of intense or difficult feelings. But if there is too much similarity, the analytic experience threatens to be too nearly a repetition of earlier experiences, which could preclude recognizing the transference as transference. The analysis may then break down, the patient either leaving treatment for safety – or seeking refuge in renewed defences against this further trauma now being re-enacted in the analysis. Some similarity is necessary to sustain the transference-illusion (and this will always be found and used by the patient unless there are manoeuvres by the therapist to prevent it) but sufficient difference is also necessary if the experience is not to become traumatic in itself.

I shall now give examples of both kinds of failure in analytic work with patients.

Example 5.3

A therapist in supervision with me confessed to feeling irritable with a patient who kept on complaining about her mother: she felt very identified with the mother of this complaining child. In her countertransference response to this patient she was becoming alienated from her patient's experience, due to a failure in empathy. The patient, therefore, could not get beyond feeling stuck in her therapy with a therapist who was being perceived as 'just like' her irritable mother.

The problem relationship being complained of here was being brought directly into the therapy: it was not merely being talked about. However, until this was understood, the patient's transference experience had remained too real to be analysed. The patient was once again in the presence of a mother-person who was failing to recognize the extent to which she had been shutting off from the patient's feelings. The traumatic degree of similarity between the therapist and the mother had continued to block this therapy.

The patient may, however, have been prompting her therapist (as with her mother) to recognize that she had a resistance to being truly in touch with what the patient was feeling. Therefore, the therapist had to restore a sufficient sense of difference between herself as therapist and herself as the transference-mother before the patient's experience of the transference could be analysed. Antipathy had to give way to empathy. With this recovery the therapy could proceed more freely.

In the next example the therapist (at least manifestly) had seemed to be different from the patient's parents.

Example 5.4

A male patient came into analysis because he had come to realize that there was something he had never been able to deal with during his previous therapy: he still had difficulty with anger – his own and other people's. In his analysis it appeared that this patient's previous therapist had always been too nice to him for it to be possible to be angry with her. He reported the following interchange, which took place when he discussed the possibility of his going back into therapy with her. The patient had said: 'I could never be *angry* with you.' To this the therapist had apparently replied: 'Was there really so much to be angry about?' The patient now realized that his anger had regularly been deflected during that therapy, the therapist thus preventing him from using her analytically in any negative transference. The patient felt that his anger had been treated as unjustified – much as it had been by his parents. It had not been accepted as belonging to the transference.

In the subsequent analysis, it was possible to work through the anger because the analyst was able to tolerate being used by the patient to represent the mother or father, towards whom he still felt very angry, with the analyst surviving the experience of being battered with much that had remained unresolved from the patient's childhood: it was crucial that he could cope with direct expressions of anger. There was evidence to suggest that the previous therapist had been attempting to be a better parent, in trying to be someone who deserved gratitude rather than anger. Because of this, the therapist had unwittingly become traumatically like the patient's actual parents, who had likewise behaved as if there could be no valid occasion for this child to be angry with them. Analysis of the negative transference had therefore not been possible for this patient with that therapist.

From the viewpoint of the therapist, these two examples may seem to be quite different. But, when viewed from the perspective of a patient's unconscious perception, they are actually very similar.

The therapist in *example 5.3* had become too much like the patient's mother; but she was aware of being discomforted by the irritation that her patient was regularly evoking in her, and she was seeking help in supervision with this difficulty. The therapist in *example 5.4* seems to have made efforts to be actively different from the patient's parents, and the patient was consciously grateful to her until he recognized the unresolved problems with anger.

The point that I am trying to illustrate in *example 5.4* is that any attempt at 'being the better parent' has the effect of deflecting, even seducing, a patient from using the analyst or therapist in a negative transference.

The 'as if' relationship

These two examples illustrate how important it is to preserve the 'as if' quality of the analytic relationship. It is this illusion that allows a patient to re-experience in the transference whatever aspects of earlier relationships are being brought into the analysis, *as if* the analyst really were the original person to whom the patient is currently feeling related. Therefore, when trauma is being brought into the transference, it is the illusion of realness that accounts for the transference experience being so immediate. Paradoxically, if this is not to become traumatic too, there needs to be an adequate sense of safety in the analytic 'holding' for it to be tolerable for the patient also to re-experience extremes of unsafety in the transference. Only thus can a patient find a viable security amidst the transference illusion of trauma re-experienced, without which there will not be room for the patient to 'play' with that experience: an important part of working-through.

Of course, if a traumatic similarity is too pronounced, whether manifest or latent, there may be no analytic space within which to analyse this as transference. From the patient's viewpoint it is then no longer experienced as transference but as real repetition. This cannot be analysed. It must first be remedied (if it can be) so that the potential space (Winnicott 1971: 100–10) of the analytic relationship is re-established. Only thus can a patient 'create' such transference as can at that moment be tolerated.

If, however, a therapist insists on being experienced as different from the original object(s) (*example 5.4*) there can be no analysable transference in that area of relating. At best there can only be 'charismatic cure', which evokes change by seduction. And, when that difference is based upon defensive behaviour by the therapist, the repetition becomes more insidious – because it is concealed. It may then continue to be beyond the conscious awareness of either party, and so remain not dealt with.

Silent trauma

What we can also learn from the examples just given is that there are times when the analytic experience itself develops into trauma. This can happen when the patient senses something wrong in the analytic relationship that is not being dealt with, as in *example 5.3* where the therapist had been unempathic because of feeling irritable; or when there is something more radically wrong that cannot readily be dealt with, as in *example 5.4* when the therapist was unable to accept her patient's angry feelings. In each of these cases, whilst the therapist's own behaviour remained unattended to, the analytic process was being deflected or hindered. Patients do not always regard this kind of failure as traumatic, but the effects upon the analytic work can be long-lasting. To this extent, therefore, I regard this as silent trauma, fitting the definition of trauma with which we started.

There are other cases where the patient becomes more obviously traumatized by the experience of therapy or analysis, but for reasons that are often not at all clear. In these cases, the childhood may not have been clearly traumatic, except perhaps cumulatively over a long period of time. The behaviour of the analyst, likewise, may not be significantly traumatic in any of the ways so far described; and yet the patient becomes unable to work in the analysis.

I believe that this hold-up in an analysis can sometimes be provoked by aspects of the analytic setting, or by the analyst's way of working. For instance, if any particular style of analysis is rigidly adhered to, it may take much longer for the analyst to recognize when problems arising in an analysis are due to the patient's response to the analyst's way of working. Analysts, therefore, have to be careful that they do not hold too strongly to their own clinical style as there is a risk that they might rationalize as *technique* their own character traits such as rigidity or having to be right; some patients may then find problems in their analysis which the analyst cannot see as directly related to him/herself. Thus, a patient's behaviour may be due to desperation about a communication failure in the analysis, but it can be mistaken for resistance. It then becomes much harder for the patient to offer corrective cues (Casement 1985; Langs 1978). That is why it is important to have a technique that allows room for unconscious prompting by the patient. The possibility of movement in the analysis can then be restored.

I wish now to give two examples where patients were temporarily stuck in their analyses with me. In each case the problem turned out to be due to traumatic similarities between my way of working and the way that each patient had experienced a parent. Renewed progress became possible only when the reasons for stalemate had been recognized and dealt with. This required some flexibility in technique.

Example 5.5

This clinical sequence is from work with a patient early in my analytic career. A female patient, Mrs G as I shall call her, often used to complain about her parents, who had separated and divorced by the time she was seven: she was an only child. She described her mother as someone who was distant and unresponsive, who thought she always knew best, and who frequently saw faults in others but never in herself. Her mother could not tolerate criticism, and if Mrs G ever made perceptive comments about her she would be accused of being out of her mind: 'You must be crazy even to think such things of your own mother' would be a typical response. Her father was mostly absent from her life.

In her analysis Mrs G became very stuck. She would often lie silent and paralysed. Interpretations, even if accepted, did not help. Instead, she came to feel persecuted by any attempt of mine to interpret; she experienced this as my trying to 'see into her'. She once remarked: 'My mother used to say that she knew what I was thinking, and it often felt as if she did.'

The patient increasingly came to see the analytic relationship as traumatically similar to her experience of her parents. For instance, her mother (like a caricature analyst) used not to answer personal questions; instead, she would often parry with other questions, or she would query the patient's motives in asking such questions of her. The father, by contrast, remained a shadowy presence in the background. Mrs G thus came to see me as just like these parents. This was very difficult to treat simply as transference as these parents had, in some respects, behaved much as I then used to think analytic technique required of me to behave.

For this patient, therefore, the analytic setting and the usual techniques of analysis had *in themselves* become a traumatic repetition of her childhood relationships. As a result she became unable to recognize the transference dimension within this context of sameness. She had to discover a sufficient difference between me and her parents before she could resume working analytically with me.

I shall not describe in any detail the prolonged period of analysis during which this problem was being worked out. In essence, I had to discover ways of being more flexible with the patient. For instance, when Mrs G asked me a personal question she used to defend herself from any rebuff by saying: 'Of course, I know you won't answer that.' Sometimes, to her surprise, I chose to give her a straight answer. Also, when she had accurately read what I was thinking or feeling, I would sometimes affirm her impression rather than fend it off.

In ways like these Mrs G was able to elicit responses from me that she had not been able to get from her parents, and which she likewise did not expect from an analyst. Naturally, I had to watch carefully for repercussions from such self-revelations, but the gains in the analysis clearly outweighed the occasional difficulties that arose from this openness.

Mrs G eventually became able to discover for herself the paradox of transference, becoming able to explore the recurring sense of sameness within a growing awareness of difference in the analytic relationship. Gradually she recovered from the paralysing conviction that I was really just the same as her parents. She could then use me more freely in the transference *to represent* the relationship difficulties that she had had with each of her parents, which continued to be the paramount focus of the analytic work. This had not been deflected by the evidence of difference: it was this difference, in the end, that had made it possible to analyse the patient's transference experience.

In the following clinical sequence, I can illustrate something more of this discovery of difference.

Example 5.6

As an infant, Mr H had often been left to choke upon his own crying. He used then to expérience his mother as having abandoned him. A phantasy was subsequently developed whereby this abandonment had been seen as related to the intensity of his need for his mother's attention. The more intensely he needed this – the more sure he became that he would be abandoned.

Silences in the analysis were frequently experienced as abandonment or retaliation. This did not mean that I therefore felt this patient should be protected from all silences; but it was clear I should monitor the degree of anxiety that he could tolerate – and space my silences accordingly.

A technical problem here was that Mr H also expected me to be unable to tolerate the intensity of his anxiety and his anger. Therefore, if I responded too quickly to a silence I was seen as afraid of his violent reaction to my silences. Gradually, I came to realize that the transference experience sometimes became so total for Mr H that the therapeutic alliance was in jeopardy or seemed to be entirely absent.

Eventually, Mr H pointed me towards a way of beginning to deal with this problem. He began to complain that the lights in my room made his eyes ache. Would I please turn off the light in front of him during his sessions? I then recalled a discussion, with Dr Martin James, of his paper 'Premature ego development' (James 1960). In this discussion, Martin James had made the following statement: 'All analysis has to be conducted within the omnipotence of the patient, which has to be challenged sensitively and very very cautiously.' He later illustrated this by giving an example of a patient who needed him 'to provide the basic sameness of the initial mothering, within the analytic situation, before the patient could tolerate change and thus begin to grow'.

The impression I had of my patient's mother was that she had become prematurely unavailable to him. I, therefore, did not think there had been an adequate preparation for this sudden distance. There had been no 'progressive failure to adapt' (Winnicott 1965: 87). Maybe, then, Mr H needed me to provide symbolic evidence of my basic sameness, as a thread of continuity by which he could hold on to me (as someone still controlled by him), whilst he was experiencing intensely violent feelings towards me, as towards the mother who had remained unresponsive to him even when he had been most needy.

For about six months I regularly turned off the offending light. In doing this I was responding to what I regarded as a need that should be met. I was not simply trying to placate the patient; rather, my flexibility here signified a difference from his parents that freed him sufficiently to rage at me in the transference – for instance, over my silences or my failures to understand. Inevitably, I sometimes forgot to turn off the light. I had then to pay for that too, and in no uncertain terms, the patient using that tangible failure to rage at me, as against failures in the early holding environment, in ways so well described by Winnicott (1958: 281; 1965: 258).

As we worked through what was required in this phase of the analysis, Mr H became able to relinquish his token of control. When he was ready, *he* told *me* one day that he could cope with the light being left on. This meant he could begin to use me as someone able to survive his rages. My separateness from him could then be more clearly established, and he became able to explore further his murderous attacks upon me in dreams and in his waking thoughts.

The corrective emotional experience[3]

It is a seductive idea that what our patients might be needing, for recovery from past bad experience, is an analyst willing to provide opportunities for good experiences as a substitute for those that had been lacking in childhood. But things are not so easily changed in the internal world of the patient.

The analytic 'good object' is not someone better than the original object: it is someone who survives being treated as a 'bad object'. By surviving I mean neither collapsing under that experience nor retaliating because of it (see Winnicott 1971: 91).

Example 5.7

In my chapter 'Analytic holding under pressure' (Casement 1985: 155–67) I describe a patient, Mrs B, who reached a point where she felt she could not possibly go on with her analysis unless I would let her hold my hand if the reliving of an early trauma became too unbearable. I will not go over the clinical sequence in full here; but, as the case illustrates my present argument most clearly, I shall draw out a few of its significant features and discuss it in a slightly different way.

At the age of eleven months Mrs B had been badly burned, and six months later her scars were operated on under a local anaesthetic. In the course of her analysis, she began to experience me as the surgeon who had operated on her, and became utterly terrified of me. During that operation her mother, who was holding her hands, had fainted. In telling me that she might need to hold my hand, she was appealing to me to be available to her as a mother who would protect her from the transference experience of me as the surgeon.

Under pressure, and aware of the extremity of her early experience, I agreed that she might need this possibility. However, over the ensuing weekend I gave much thought to the implications for Mrs B if I offered myself to be a 'better mother', and I realized that this could become a collusion with her wish to avoid the worst part of her experience by not facing it *as it was*.

The patient's subsequent use of me in the transference came to include the experience of not being physically held – after her mother had fainted. I then had to be able to face the impact of the patient's feelings from that time. And, eventually, Mrs B could find that I had survived in my own right; not by some manipulation of the clinical situation, nor by her continuing to protect me from what she experienced as the worst within herself. Only thus was I able to relieve her of the unconscious dread that nobody could ever bear to be in touch with her most intense feelings as they had been at the time of the original trauma.

As Winnicott says (1965: 258), this was something very different from the notion of cure by corrective emotional experience. A key distinction here is that the experience, unconsciously being looked for, was quite different from anything I could have prescribed for the patient. It was *she* who had found the analytic experience that was in the end most therapeutically effective. *It had not been provided for her.* What had been provided was a sufficient security in the analytic 'holding' for her to bear to remember the early trauma of not having been held; and now, her remembering (by re-experiencing that trauma in the transference) could be in the presence of someone against whom she could safely rage – as at the mother who had become absent through fainting.

Much later in the analysis the patient reflected upon that time. She said of this: 'What was so important was not just that you survived: *it was that you survived – but only just.*' It had therefore been vital to her that she had seen evidence of my being truly in touch with the intensity of her distress, for it had been that which had contributed to her mother's fainting. But it had also been essential that I had managed to find a way of staying with her most difficult feelings from that trauma – that I had not deflected these by trying to be the 'better mother'.

Conclusion

When we are treating a patient who has been traumatized, it is inevitable that the traumatic experience will eventually come to be represented in the transference – if we do not deflect this or prevent it. The re-experiencing of trauma then turns out to be a subtle blend of truth and illusion: it combines the realities both of the analytic situation and of the patient's internal world, where unconscious memories of trauma are still dynamically present. The resulting illusion, of the past and the present being powerfully experienced as the 'same', is based upon an unconscious set of experiences that have remained timeless – because in the unconscious there is no sense of time (Freud 1915: 187). A similar set of experiences in the present thus comes to represent the original trauma.

In learning to distinguish *the present* from *the past that spills into the present*, a patient has to find sufficient difference between the analytic relationship now and the situation as it had been at earlier times of trauma. This means that the analyst has to be careful not to be disturbingly similar to the patient's primary objects of the past; but it also turns out to be crucial that it is the patient who discovers the necessary difference – this should not be actively demonstrated by the analyst. Likewise, any similarity that may come to be used to represent trauma should also be found by the patient: in no way should this be consciously introduced by the analyst.

If the analytic process is not to be impeded or distorted, the analyst has to be careful not to influence or direct the patient. This means that he should not deliberately provide experience that is thought to be 'good for the patient', as suggested by advocates of cure by emotional experience. But what *can* be provided is a security within the analytic relationship that allows the patient to feel understood, sensitively responded to, and analytically 'held', by an analyst who can tolerate what is yet to come in the course of the analysis, without collapse or retaliation.

Therefore, when a patient is prompting the analyst to depart from classical technique, particularly if it is being rigidly adhered to, this need not always be seen as seductive or manipulative. The patient may be searching for a more viable balance between the similarities in the analytic relationship (that represent trauma) and a sufficient difference (that alone can provide the necessary security for the analysis to continue). It is the balance here that matters.

Chapter six

The meeting of needs in psychoanalysis[1]

The process of change in psychoanalysis cannot be explained only in terms of the interpretive work of understanding unconscious content. The part played by the meeting of unmet needs is also taken into account – through the provision of a 'second chance' to attend to the effects of trauma and to negotiate outstanding developmental tasks. The essential differences between this meeting of needs in psychoanalysis and any attempt at providing a 'corrective emotional experience' are also considered.

Introduction

I have already indicated that in my view corrective emotional experience cannot be *provided* for a patient by the analyst or therapist. Here it is worth considering what patients *find* within the analytic encounter that can, of itself, be therapeutic. In particular I wish to draw attention to some of the many ways in which needs from childhood recur in the course of analysis or therapy. This re-presentation of need by a patient is, I believe, unconsciously in the service of a continuing search for attention to needs that have remained unmet.

First, however, I wish to remind the reader of a distinction that I regard as diagnostically necessary in relation to the issue under discussion: between 'libidinal demands', which cannot be gratified in any analytic psychotherapy without risking a serious disturbance of the analytic process, and 'needs' which cannot be frustrated without preventing growth. Winnicott (1965: ch. 4) has called these latter 'ego-needs'; in relation to later development, I have found it useful to think of them as 'growth-needs' (Winnicott 1965: 141; Casement 1985: 170–2).

Views on the concept of corrective emotional experience have been very polarized. The concept was originally proposed by

90

Alexander (Alexander *et al.* 1946; Alexander 1954), and more recently by Moberly (1985). In the latter's view, corrective emotional experience represents essentially what is therapeutic in analysis. Many others, however, have been almost entirely dismissive of Alexander's concept, because the notion of an analyst actively choosing to play a role can now be seen to be antithetical to any truly analytic process. And this difference is most particularly evident when psychoanalysis is recognized as a process with its own dynamic and sense of direction – emerging from the unconscious of the patient.

At the time when Alexander was writing, however, it was pertinent for him to be drawing attention to the therapeutic value of the emotional experience of patients in analysis. For it was already becoming clear that patients do not benefit only from insight, nor was it the experience of transference, or of transference interpretation (as in Strachey 1934), that alone brought about lasting change. Beyond the experience of transference there is much else that affects the patient in the analytic relationship, for good or for ill. We still have much to learn about the effects upon patients of the analyst's presence and manner of interpreting.

It is my contention here that some key unmet needs of a patient may be met in the course of an analysis or pyschotherapy. But I question any *deliberate* attempts at providing good experience for the patient. I believe that that can only deflect the analytic process: it does not enhance it.

Corrective emotional experience

Taken out of context, the idea of the therapeutic factor in psychoanalysis being closely related to corrective emotional experience may seem attractive. We may also find Alexander's own description of his technique superficially quite appealing:

> the main *therapeutic* result of our work is the conclusion that, in order to be relieved of his neurotic ways of feeling and acting, the patient must undergo new emotional experiences suited to undo the morbid effects of the emotional experiences of his earlier life. Other therapeutic factors – such as intellectual insight, abreaction, recollection of the past, etc. – are all subordinated to this central therapeutic principle.
>
> (Alexander *et al.* 1946: 338)

He goes on to say that the therapist has a unique opportunity 'to provide the patient with precisely that type of corrective experience which he needs for recovery'. But we may feel rather cautious when he concludes: 'It is a secondary question what technique is employed to bring it about' (Alexander *et al.* 1946: 338).

When we look more closely at this concept, and the technique advocated, we find that Alexander recommended the analyst should present the patient with deliberate provocations, selected on the basis of a 'principle of contrast', the analyst consciously choosing to respond in ways that are opposite to the manner in which the parents had behaved (Alexander 1954). And he had previously given some examples to illustrate the kind of technique he has in mind:

> If the therapist knows what kind of problem is emerging into consciousness, he will find it simple to elicit such reactions deliberately. He may, for example, praise a patient for therapeutic progress in order to bring out a latent guilt feeling about receiving the father's approval. Or he may express approval of a friend of the patient's in order to bring out latent jealousy.
>
> (Alexander *et al.* 1946: 83)

He does, however, admit that the response to such a provocation may be 'of such intensity that it is difficult to control'. And he goes on to say:

> What is even more important, if the therapist has, in fact, deliberately provoked such a reaction, it may later be much more difficult to convince the patient that his reaction is really a repetition of an earlier pattern and not a quite natural reaction to the therapist's behavior.
>
> (Alexander *et al.* 1946: 83)

Alexander acknowledges here one of the problems with his proposed technique, but knowing the difficulty does not mean that an analysis of the transference can then be convincingly restored, especially when there has clearly been some manipulation of the patient by the analyst.

So, in thinking about a possible rehabilitation of the concept of corrective emotional experience, we have to remember that this term has a bad history. And it is questionable whether the concept can be altogether separated from its reputation.

Some needs of childhood most relevant to analysis

It is especially in relation to regression that analysts have to decide how to handle early emotional states, as these are represented within the analytic relationship. But it will be my thesis here that many of these early needs are met as a matter of course in the analyst's usual responses to a patient. They do not necessarily require any particular alteration of analytic technique so much as a sensitivity to the changing needs of the patient and an adequate responsiveness to them on the part of the analyst.

As background to a comparison between the needs of early life and needs expressed by patients, I wish to review some of the needs of infancy (and childhood) that are most likely to be represented at different stages of regression and progression in an analysis.

We know that an infant needs to be provided with warmth and security, in the presence of the mother and in her absence; needs to be securely held; needs to have the consistent care of a mother (or mother substitute) who has an empathic understanding of the infant's various indications of what is needed; needs to be fed but also to be given space in which to find the breast that feeds; needs a mother who can tolerate being 'used' (in the pre-concern phase of development) without the mother either collapsing or retaliating; needs a mother who can intuitively accept the infant's initially 'omnipotent' control of her; needs a mother who can tolerate (at least) and even enjoy (without exploiting) the infant's capacity for an excited relationship to the breast – and (later) to her as a whole person; needs a mother who is at first able to be maximally available to her infant but who becomes progressively less available and less controlled by the infant's demands – as development makes possible a greater toleration of frustration; and, throughout, the infant needs to be able to discover his/her capacity to light up the mother's face – for here is to be found the fundamental basis of self-image and self-esteem.

As children grow, what they need of the mother (and father) continues to change. Manageable degrees of separation from the mother need to become an integral part of life. And, when triangular relationships are discovered, the feelings related to Oedipal development need also to be found to be manageable by the mother and father, and eventually by the child. Also, from the Oedipal phase onwards, children who are growing into an awareness of their sexuality need to feel that this can be affirmed by the parents, as valued and not to be exploited: they also need to discover that their sexuality can be accepted as healthy and manageable, and does not have to be ignored or treated as bad or dangerous. And at various stages, throughout childhood and particularly in adolescence, there needs to be the possibility of confrontation with a parent (or parents) able to survive the battering that can accompany a child's demonstration that it has an autonomous mind that is being tested in opposition to the parents' wishes (see Winnicott 1971: ch. 11). Of course, there is much else that is needed in childhood but this sample will suffice for the purpose of the present discussion.

Some parallels in the analytic relationship

Omnipotent control

Many patients need to be allowed to establish a provisional omnipotence over the analyst, in the early stages of an analysis, as a basis for primitive security; and this should be challenged only by degrees, and only as the patient becomes ready to relinquish this form of control over the analyst (see *example 5.6*).

In practice what does this mean? If the analyst is going to be found by the patient as someone to be trusted, with the sometimes quite terrifying (because so intense) feelings that can accompany regression, the analyst needs to be able to maintain a delicate balance of being controlled by the patient without being rendered impotent. This balance will not be achieved if the analyst is too actively insistent upon preserving a separateness from the patient, nor will it be if the analyst remains either silently detached or too frequently intervening with interpretations. There has to be a time during which the patient can gradually 'discover' the analyst in ways that belong to where the patient is in the emerging transference. Where, developmentally, the patient might be in this process is not always clear straight away.

Space

Patients, like infants and children of whatever age, need a sense of space which protects them from the experience of being impinged upon by the environment (or by the analyst). The analytic environment can then be discovered gradually as a patient becomes ready to find this and ready to be relating to it. (I return to this issue in Chapter 10.) I therefore think it is presumptuous and intrusive when some analysts interpret *right from the start of an analysis* in terms of some assumed primitive transference. What is active so early in treatment is usually a more general transference to the *unknown* of the analyst or sometimes to the *known* of the analytic situation – particularly when there has been an earlier experience of therapy or analysis. It is only gradually, in my opinion, that more specific transferences begin to emerge.

In this respect, patients could be compared with a compass needle. Even a very faintly magnetized needle, if freely suspended, will eventually find its own magnetic North – thus revealing its potential for direction-seeking. But if some large object, with its own magnetic properties, is too near to the needle it will only point to that. Some analysts may disturb the emergence of more individual transferences by too quickly regarding themselves as the assumed focus of a patient's life and internal world.

The need to be 'fed'

It is quite common for analysts to regard the analytic relationship as a feeding one, and for the patient's difficulties in feeding to become a focus for interpretation. The feeding here is symbolic and the 'food' offered is in the form of interpretations. Very occasionally one hears of exceptions to this. For instance, Freud reports feeding one of his patients, the Rat Man (Freud 1909: 303), and sometimes one hears of an analyst giving food to an anorexic patient. But this is always a compromise which usually indicates some anxiety that what is being offered analytically may not be enough. And if the analyst takes over responsibility for some part of a patient's life this can be read by the patient as an implicit communication that the analyst may be prepared to take over other aspects of care-giving too. This can create considerable difficulties unless the analyst (like Winnicott) is prepared to meet the demands and expectations that are likely to be stimulated by such 'acting in' by the analyst.[2]

It is also important that patients are left free to discover the analyst as 'breast' or as 'feeding mother' in their own time. In this respect the analyst needs to tolerate what Winnicott speaks of as the 'period of hesitation' (Winnicott 1958: 53), allowing the patient to use the analyst as someone who is there to be found – a presence that is neither intrusively present nor traumatically absent to the patient. Thus the patient can begin to reach out, to find and to use the analyst in whatever way – with a timing that belongs to the patient's internal world and which corresponds to the patient's readiness to relate. If a mother presents her baby with the breast only when it suits her, regardless of the rhythm of the baby's needs, she may get a lifeless compliance. Similarly, if we ignore a patient's rhythm, the relationship to the analyst is in danger of being based upon compliance – the analyst being experienced as an impingement that threatens the patient's internal world and true self. What follows then can all too easily fall into further false-self relating. Often, this has been the patient's life-long problem already. Therefore, when an analyst gets drawn into being too active, becoming a presence that impinges upon the patient, it is useful to review this interaction for the diagnostic clues that may be indicated. Sometimes, through the process of 'unconscious role-responsiveness', the analyst may be being drawn into a re-enactment of some central aspect of the patient's past experience. But this will not be recognized as such if the analyst's own style of working is already prone to be over-active and potentially impinging upon the patient.

The need for warmth and security

A patient needs to feel securely held in an analysis, but the manner of this holding has to take into account the fact that the analyst is dealing with *the child within the adult* – not just a child – however regressed the patient may be.[3] So the analytic precept of abstinence continues to be crucially important here.

When, as we sometimes hear, an analyst rationalizes a physical holding of a patient, we cannot be sure how the patient will experience and interpret that holding. On the one hand, a literal holding will often, at some level, be experienced by the patient as sexual. On the other hand, it can become a collusive step by the analyst whereby the distinction between the symbolic and the concrete is confused. And, once this distinction has been lost, the analytic relationship may then become changed by the patient's hope that other gratifications may be granted, which sometimes are yearned for and phantasized. The patient may then be deprived of the analytic space which is so essential if there is to be a freedom to 'play' with various aspects of relating without having to be anxious about these becoming realized between him/her and the analyst.

A patient feels secure through appropriate interpretation. Of this Winnicott wrote:

A correct and well-timed interpretation in an analytic

treatment gives a sense of being held physically that is more real (to the non-psychotic) than if a real holding or nursing had taken place. Understanding goes deeper and by understanding, shown by the use of language, the analyst holds physically in the past, that is, at the time of the need to be held, when love meant physical care and adaptation.

(Winnicott 1988: 61–2)

This need of the child in the adult (for holding) has to be met, and clinical experience repeatedly shows that, with very few exceptions, it is more productive in the end for this need to be met analytically. However, Winnicott's analysis of Margaret Little (see note 2) might be one of these exceptions.

Consistency and firmness

Another way in which patients are able to discover a sense of being secure is through the analyst being found to be consistent and reliable. Here, too, deep needs from earliest infancy are met within the analytic relationship. It is therefore of utmost importance to the patient that the analyst keep to the arrangements made, with as little change or interruption as possible, and for the analyst also to work with the patient in ways that are consistent.

Paradoxically, a part of the consistency that a patient needs from the analyst is that of *empathic responsiveness to changing needs*. This may require the analyst sometimes to be adapting to the patient rather than remaining rigidly the same. In this responsiveness the analyst again parallels early mothering. For after a period of omnipotent control of the analyst, a patient needs eventually to find that a firmness is also available that can withstand testing – even severe testing – and which can later be used for the purposes of confrontation. The analyst can thus be found, after all, to be separate from the patient.

Being used by the patient

When earlier differentiation has been disturbed, or has remained incomplete, the patient has a second chance in an analysis to work through the developmental tasks that belong to that process. But this is only possible if the analyst's separateness can be gradually discovered by the patient beyond the more regressed use of the analyst during which he/she may have been experienced as but an extension of the patient.

This more primitive use of the analyst, as described by Winnicott in his paper 'The use of an object' (Winnicott 1971: ch. 6), is possible only when the analyst can tolerate the patient relating in ways that belong to very early stages in life, in particular to the stage that Winnicott (1958: 265) describes as 'pre-ruth' (ruthless = without concern). In this experience a patient unconsciously seeks to discover an object that can survive being 'destroyed'. But this typical sequence in analysis will be greatly disturbed, or even prevented, if the analyst is too quick to interpret this 'destroying' of the analyst as sadistic – or as symptomatic of something in the patient to be eliminated – rather than to be lived with and worked through.

Aspects of self-experience[4]

In the way of infants with mothers, so patients' views of themselves can be deeply affected by the way they feel the analyst relates to them. For this reason, I have come to think of those aspects of the psychoanalytic experience that have this effect upon patients as being related to self-experience. I therefore regard self-esteem and self-image as products of self-experience – *reflecting how others have related to the Self*. In analysis, therefore, we need to recognize the many ways in which analysts affect their patients' self-experience through their ways of interpreting and through the nature of their responses to the patients' communications.

Feelings experienced as manageable

A most important self-experience for many patients is when they discover that the analyst is able to accept the expression of difficult feelings as a communication. Feelings can then begin to lose the associations of a life-time, either as feared or as something to be ashamed of. There are many occasions in analysis when patients discover, perhaps for the first time, that feelings – however intense – can be communicated and can be understood; they do not have to be repressed any more. There is much therapeutic gain for a patient when the analyst is seen to be surviving in the face of intense feelings that are being expressed by the patient, when previous figures in the patient's life had either collapsed or retaliated.

The value of the analyst's survival is most particularly impressive when he/she is working with projective identification as a communication from the patient. Feelings that could not previously be managed by the patient alone can then be found to have been communicated to the analyst, who is made to experience these feelings instead of the patient. Projective identification may unconsciously aim to get rid of unmanageable feelings but it also serves to get help with feelings. And, when that help is forthcoming in the analysis, a patient will have the experience of finding a response that had been looked for in the past but which had been significantly lacking from the key figures of childhood.

The implications of care

There are many other gains in self-experience for patients to be found in the analyst's attention and presence: of being a person who is taken seriously; who is listened to carefully; over whom the analyst takes trouble at many different levels of communication. Patients can sense when the analyst is in touch with what they are experiencing, and they can be deeply affected when they realize that they are with someone who is surviving what they are communicating, when they did not believe anyone could survive that; and much else. In all these respects patients have opportunities to discover fresh aspects of themselves, and a different self-image, reflected in the analyst's responses.

Through the experience of these parallels in the analytic relationship, a patient may also rediscover something of the experience of the mother's face as the first 'mirror', in which the Self can be reflected as good, as lively and to be enjoyed.[5]

There is, however, a problem about change that is brought about through the patient's experience of the analytic relationship. Sometimes, an experience that may have seemed helpful to the patient turns out not to be lasting. The first of the following examples is intended to illustrate this problem.

Clinical examples

It is not enough to be a 'better parent'

Example 6.1

A female patient aged twenty-six (Miss J), who had already been in therapy some years before, sought further help in analysis. She acknowledged that she had gained a lot from her former therapist – in fact, in that earlier therapy, Miss J had been helped out of a prolonged depression and she had begun to find new purpose in life. For the most part, therefore, she had remained grateful to her therapist but she had since begun to feel that there was something important missing in that therapy.

It transpired that, some two years into the earlier therapy, Miss J had continued to regard her life as meaningless. One day, her therapist had apparently said to her: 'But there is a lot you could do with your life – you have a lot to give to others.' Now, for someone who had felt starved of affirmation, such words had been like nectar and the patient had felt flattered; and Miss J told me that she had been very moved by her therapist's affirmation of her. So, when her therapist later offered the further suggestion that she might feel more fulfilled if she had a job working with people, Miss J felt strongly motivated to enquire into the possibility of a change in her career. She subsequently applied for social work training and, from then, her life had seemed to take on a new sense of direction. However, after that therapy had ended, this patient had found herself once again questioning the meaning of her life. Her depression had returned, which is why she had asked for analysis.

A significant dream

Early in her analysis with me Miss J recounted *a dream from her earlier therapy*:

> I had been projecting a photograph of grasses on to a screen.
> To my surprise and intense excitement this photograph
> appeared to be three-dimensional. I then fetched my mother to
> look at this but she could not see anything unusual about it.
> My sister, however, was able to see the real-life quality of the
> photograph; but she then rearranged the grasses and they
> began to fall to pieces. The picture which had been so
> remarkable became totally destroyed.

Miss J further commented: 'I awoke from that dream beside myself with anger.'

The previous therapist had interpreted this dream as a projection of the hidden good in the patient, representing herself as having a value she had failed to own because it had not previously been adequately affirmed by others. The mother's not noticing and the sister's interference both seemed to be in character with Miss J's experience of them. The therapist's interpretation therefore had a great impact on the patient, and she had continued to regard this dream, and the work around it, as a central gain in that therapy.

However, what of Miss J's later experience? She had finished the social work training and was beginning her new career, but she reported that she felt a fraud when seeing clients; she didn't know why. Even though her previous therapist had clearly helped her to feel more positively about herself, that benefit had not lasted. I therefore came to wonder whether it could have been that Miss J had identified with a view of herself that seemed to have been accepted from an idealized therapist, which had however failed to become truly autonomous. If that were so, it might explain why the change in self-image had collapsed when Miss J no longer had the continuing presence and influence of the person who had expressed a belief in her.[6]

Discussion

I think that this brief example raises some important issues. Providing a patient with an experience that was meant to be helpful often does not produce the therapeutic results that might be expected. Why does this attempt fail?

I think we get some clues here in the patient's much valued dream and the therapist's interpretation of it. What had previously been picked up from this had been the disowned (not recognized) good aspects of the patient that were seen in projection (the three-dimensional photograph), and that interpretation had its own validity. But what seems not to have been picked up then was the unconscious prompt to the therapist which can also be seen in that dream, for it represents the patient as having been interfered with. The thoughts of changing her career, which had been prompted by the therapist's interventions shortly before this dream, might unconsciously have been recognized as originating from just such an interference. In addition we find a reference to the now life-like arrangement of grasses going to pieces. Perhaps this had been an unconscious metaphor for the false-self adjustment which was resulting from the patient fitting in with her therapist's suggestions. Later, when she was asking for analysis, Miss J had consciously begun to recognize that something was going to pieces in herself.

The very fact that Miss J felt a need to seek further analytic help grew out of her becoming aware of how precarious had been the adjustment in her self-esteem through the previous therapist's influence. It only later became clear that Miss J's earlier life had been dogged by many false-self adjustments, whereby she had offered changes in how she was in an attempt to please (or placate) parents and significant others.

The previous therapist appeared to have offered herself as a 'better parent'. This could have seemed justified as a corrective emotional experience, using Alexander's 'principle of contrast'. But what was most important in the later analysis was found in the patient's discovery that she could eventually use me to represent precisely those ways in which she had been let down in the past, as with her parents and her sister. Feelings about those early relationships, which had continued to preoccupy her and which she had expected to remain unmanageable, could then be re-experienced and worked through in the transference relationship. In particular, Miss J discovered that her explosive and previously repressed anger could be allowed expression in the analysis, and that this did not lead to either the collapse or the retaliation she had been accustomed to expect in her earlier relationships but led to a new vitality in herself and in her approach to life.

In the course of this analysis Miss J also recovered a freedom to choose whether to continue with her new career or to do something different. She no longer had to please her therapist or her analyst.

A different use of contrast

Example 6.2

Mrs K, a woman in her early thirties, had come into analysis from a mental hospital. She had been briefly admitted there after the birth of her second child – a girl. Her first child was a boy.

I soon learned from Mrs K that she had been intensely jealous of her brother, born when she was two, and that her mother was then said to have become unable to cope with her. As a result, Mrs K had been lodged with her grandmother for a while, the family hoping that this would give her mother time to settle down with the new baby, her brother. When she returned home she had become very withdrawn, which was easier for her mother to manage. Inwardly she was feeling unwanted and very unhappy, but she no longer felt able to turn to her mother for help with that unhappiness.

It soon became evident that Mrs K had felt the birth of her second child to be a repetition of her own childhood experience. She had identified with the baby girl as representing herself just born. But, at another level, she also identified with her mother of that time – the mother who now had two children. (It transpired that her mother had suffered a post-puerperal depression after Mrs K's birth.) So there was now a powerful spilling of the past into the present, and Mrs K felt as if she was about to lose her mother all over again. Her panic and withdrawal into hospital therefore had partly represented an 'identification with aggressor', by means of which she was passing on to her new-born baby something of her own experience of desertion by *her* mother. Her baby, instead of herself, now became the one who lost a mother.

Mrs K began to feel some relief from gaining insight into this sequence around her daughter's birth, but the gains at first were limited because that insight continued to be split off from being experienced within the analytic relationship. However, when those conflicts did emerge in the transference, the patient's early experiences began to be re-enacted most vividly within the analysis.

The transference neurosis

When we passed into the third year of her analysis, Mrs K became obsessively concerned with problems related to my waiting-room. She felt shut out and excluded if she arrived early whilst I was seeing another patient. However, rather than protect herself from that distress by not coming so early she began to come earlier still. This also created a problem for me, as her presence in the waiting-room was felt by the patients before her to be intrusive. The end of sessions too became difficult, with Mrs K sometimes being extremely reluctant to leave.

It became clear that what was now emerging in the transference was her experience of me as the mother who was attending to another child. She became possessively jealous and very angry; she began to rage in her sessions that I should alter my schedule so that she could be protected from this distress; she should not have to be aware of other patients; and she complained that I was a bad analyst in not having more space between sessions, etc.

For several weeks it seemed as if I could not do anything right with Mrs K. No interpretation from me seemed to make any difference. Whatever I said was dismissed, argued with or ignored; and if I did not speak – that was interpreted by the patient as rejection.

The crunch came soon after my summer holiday. Upon my return Mrs K was very withdrawn. When I wondered about this, she began to complain that she felt 'shaky' and afraid that she might explode with what she was feeling inside. Then, in my second week back, Mrs K began to pour out her rage at me. 'Be honest', she shouted, 'you can't cope with me! No one can. Send me back to hospital. That's where I belong. All I'm good for is pills and electric shock treatment. Go on, ring up the hospital to come and fetch me. (Pause.) Why are you not saying anything?'

During this outburst I was aware of feeling intensely anxious. Was she right? Was it perhaps true that I could not manage her? But there were other clues. Her withdrawal after my absence reminded me of her return home after having been sent away to her grandmother. She had been two then and her brother had recently been born. She had been in analysis for two years and we had been working on this in relation to the waiting-room obsession. Nevertheless, to an almost delusional degree, *I had now become the mother of her as the two-year-old child.* And here she was bringing into the transference the feelings she'd had before, that her mother had not been able to manage, but this time she was able to give voice to them and to put them into words.

I eventually said to Mrs K: 'You are re-experiencing feelings that belong to the time when your brother was born. You therefore expect me, as your mother, to prefer other patients to you. And you assume that I will not to be able to cope with what you are feeling. So, as with her, you expect me to send you away rather than to continue to be available to you for the needs that you are bringing to me.'

Mrs K began to calm down, and she was able to leave at the end of the session without the difficulty that both she and I had anticipated.

Discussion

In this case we can see that it had not been enough for me merely to be the empathic analyst, or 'better' parent, who could help the patient to understand her reactions around the birth of her new baby. Although that interpretive work had helped to relieve some of her immediate anxiety, through her beginning to understand this better, *she still had feelings within herself that no one had been able to manage.* Her mother had not been able to attend to her needs sufficiently after her brother was born, and eventually she had been sent to her grandmother. Also, when she had become so depressed after the birth of her second baby, her doctor had felt that she could not be managed at home. He too had sent her away, this time to hospital. Those same feelings had therefore continued to haunt her as if they might at any time explode and repeat the rejections of her childhood.

Mrs K could not be helped by any experience of simple contrast between her relationship to me, and the relationship she had had to her mother. Instead, she experienced me as the mother who had rejected her. She then felt justified in expressing towards me the repressed feelings that had so dominated her since that early time.

Far from providing this patient with an experience that was designed to *contrast* with what she had experienced in her childhood, Mrs K had found her own way to use me as if I were the *same* as her mother. Only then could she find a therapeutic difference in her experience with me that could help to bring about real and lasting change. The difference was that I could tolerate being treated as if I were the rejecting mother of her early life, and I could survive being subjected to those feelings that had first been associated with that early experience of rejection.

What is therapeutic in analysis?[7]

The primary task of analysis is usually thought of as that of understanding unconscious conflict and unconscious phantasy. But, as I have already indicated, changes in self-image and self-esteem also reflect the quality of the analytic relationship. However, as *example 6.1* shows, what is therapeutic in analysis is not to be attained through any simple provision of better parenting. Patients often need to use the analyst for working through feelings about early experiences *as they had been* (see *examples 5.5* and *5.7*). It is not enough simply to have experience in the analytic relationship that might seem to be 'corrective'.

Other therapeutic benefit, however, does often develop from a patient discovering within the analytic relationship a whole range of relating that allows for stages of development to be worked through afresh, and this often includes the meeting of needs that had been insufficiently met before. This relating ranges from merging to separation, from part-object relating to whole-object relating, from a pre-concern use of the analyst to concerned relating, from hating to loving, etc. At times, the patient also needs the analyst to be capable of resonant empathy, whereby he or she can sense the patient's own most difficult or delicate feelings that are not always communicated solely in words. And when containment is needed, or confrontation, it is also important that the analyst can then respond with a firmness that can survive being tested.

An analyst is helped into these different ways of relating by the cues that emanate from a patient's unconscious search for what is necessary to meet unmet needs. By responding to these unconscious prompts, and not being afraid to follow them, an analyst can often get closer to what is appropriate for the patient at the different stages of an analysis. This can also lead to surprising results because what is most deeply needed by a patient, for recovery, is not always what the analyst might have expected.[8]

So, how does this fit in with the notion of 'corrective emotional experience'? The main difference, in my opinion, is that *therapeutic experience in analysis is found by the patient – it is not provided*. Earlier bad experience may be repeated in the search for understanding, or for 'mastery' of the anxieties related to it. But when better experience is also found in an analysis it is always important that this should have arisen spontaneously. It cannot become a matter of deliberate technique, for if it is in any way set up by the analyst it will be artificial and will eventually be experienced as false.

The pain of contrast

Finally, I wish briefly to consider an issue related to any therapeutic experience that highlights a contrast between the present and the past – particularly when a patient's childhood has been significantly bad or depriving.

It is well known that patients can become resistant to receiving, or to holding on to, good experience in the analysis. This reaction is sometimes regarded as a 'negative therapeutic reaction'. Or it is interpreted in terms of envy, on the grounds that the analyst is assumed to have something that the patient lacks – the patient being thought of as preferring to attack this rather than to accept the benefit of it.

However, I believe that there is a further way of understanding this kind of reaction: I call it 'the pain of contrast'. A negative response to experience that might appear to be 'good' seems to be an unconscious attempt by the patient to preserve childhood memories from comparison, particularly when there is a risk of exposing the depth of early deprivation or the true nature of damaging experience in childhood. Thus, when good experience is encountered, and is recognized as good, the shock to any defensively held view of childhood (as better than it was) can be very acute. Recognizing when a patient is reacting to the *pain of contrast* may help us to understand why experiences that might otherwise be thought of as good, and therefore as therapeutic for the patient, can lead some patients to be so resistant to them.

Example 6.3

A patient suddenly began crying bitterly during a session without any reason that I could identify. When eventually she was able to speak again she said: 'It is your voice. You sounded kind.' I still could not understand why this had so upset her, but a few minutes later she was able to add: 'My most common childhood memory is of my parents being harsh with me, even cruel. I cannot ever remember them being kind.'

It was with that patient I first recognized this type of reaction to good experience, and I have encountered many other examples of it since.

Conclusion

On the part of the analyst, the meeting of unmet needs in analysis is usually more incidental than deliberate. The analyst, by sticking to his/her analytic task, provides the patient with opportunities for finding what is needed – that is unconsciously looked for. The patient's experience of finding what is needed within the analytic relationship may then contribute deeply, but often silently and unseen, towards eventual therapeutic change. The part played by this kind of experience is often overlooked.

The meeting of needs *is not provided by the analyst*: it is in this fact that it is most singularly different from Alexander's own use of the corrective emotional experience. But the meeting of needs *can be found by the patient*. It then becomes possible for development and growth, which had been retarded through early environmental failure, to be resumed.

Whether or not Alexander's notion of the corrective emotional experience can be reclaimed from its history, the patient's unconscious search for necessary attention to unmet needs must be recognized as a valid process, and that search can become a powerful ally in the analytic endeavour.

Afterthought

Professional and personal needs in analysis: divergent perspectives?

I have suggested in this chapter that a key therapeutic factor in analysis is to be found in the patient's experience of the analytic relationship itself. This raises some questions about training, and how students are taught to think about the analytic process, particularly if there is a notion that what had seemed right for the trainee will be right for all other patients too.

A significant difference between the treatment experience of students in analysis and that of other patients can result from the students being concurrently involved in learning how to become an analyst or therapist. I believe that this can have the effect of tilting the focus of the analytic experience too much towards the efficacy of words (being the most tangible tool of analysis), theoretical teaching adding a further emphasis upon words and upon traditional ways of thinking about the analytic encounter.

Of course, words do have a critical function in an analysis, in identifying unconscious conflict, tracing the evolution of false connections in the mind, clarifying what belongs to whom, and providing the relief of having put into words what could not be spoken about – helping to find sense where before there had been confusion and/or non-sense. So, words are indispensable in analysis, not least in helping patients to move beyond omnipotent ideas of communication towards something more realistic. Nevertheless, we need more than words.[9]

The traditional emphasis upon the work of interpretation can lead analysts to overlook an important aspect of a patient's emotional needs: it is not always enough to have needs described and explained analytically and 'worked through' in the transference. But any idea of a fuller meeting of needs within the analytic relationship seems taboo in a training analysis, with the result that this level of experience is often withheld from patients.

Now, there is a natural tendency for students to be influenced by the standard thinking of their training body, on what counts as 'real' analysis and what counts as 'therapeutic'. There is also likely to be an implicit reliance upon the authority of the analyst, students gradually coming to accept (as their own) much of the thinking and ways of working they have experienced in the analysis. And if the clinical style of the training analyst is accepted as therapeutic, even when it has been combative and sometimes even quite sadistic, it may be identified with and acted out against others as if this were a proper part of the analytic experience. (See also Chapter 10, note 1.) There is much to be concerned about here.

What in particular may be overlooked by some students in analysis is that one of the most deeply therapeutic factors in an analysis is the extent to which a sensitive analyst parallels, in his/her way of working, the earliest relationship between a responsive mother and her infant: learning to follow the patient's cues, learning the patient's language, being open to correction by the patient when an essential communication is being missed, etc.

Interpretations do not necessarily have their deepest effect because of their content: the principal function of interpretation for many patients is in indicating the degree to which the analyst has been following, is in touch with the patient, or (maybe) not really in touch.[10] *The experience of being understood is at least as important as the detail of any insight that is conveyed.* (Students are not, however, readily encouraged to feel that they can safely prompt the training analyst to think again when there has been some misunderstanding.)

I think that, at the extremes, there are two quite different models of analysis here – but most analysts are able to combine the merits of each in some kind of balance, including both a timely firmness and an appropriate responsiveness. One model seems to stress intellectual understanding: even though affect is acknowledged as strongly linked with the gaining of insight, a premium is often placed upon trying to get the patient to understand his/her unconscious communications 'correctly'. The other model more clearly acknowledges the value of a patient's emotional experience in the analysis, insight being *discovered* with the patient rather than being *given to* the patient.[11]

Chapter seven

Unconscious hope[1]

When behaviour is recognized as communication this can often be seen to contain cues for the care-giving world, indicating unmet needs and an unconscious search for these to be more adequately attended to. This may be an important factor in the analytic process as well as in other walks of life.

Introduction

Having focused upon the meeting of needs in psychoanalysis in the previous chapter, I now wish to consider some of the ways in which these needs are indicated – in life as well as in analysis. I shall therefore be taking a fresh look at some familiar phenomena, developmental and clinical, in order to examine an aspect of these that seldom gets any attention. I shall be speaking of hope.[2] I am not thinking of hope that is conscious, nor of hope which is projected – when one person may 'carry' hope on behalf of another (though I shall touch upon that); nor am I thinking of the unrealistic expectations sometimes attributed to the 'trans-formational object' (Bollas 1987). I am suggesting that there may be an unconscious search (or hope) for what is needed to meet unmet needs; and that parents and analysts are given clues to what is needed in behaviour, and even in some forms of defence or pathology.

I shall be focusing here upon hope that is essentially healthy, even if it may later be expressed through pathology. To that end I find it useful to make a distinction between different forms of unconscious communication. When communication is intentional, even if unconscious, it has the active aim of reaching out to another person. By contrast, incidental communication (not knowingly intended) may also indicate unmet need, but more obliquely.

110

Precursors of hope

It is hard to tell at what point in development we can think of hope beginning to be established. I shall therefore begin with the meeting of basic needs, such as the infant's need for secure holding, for feeding, for being played with and enjoyed, and the over-all need that responses to the infant's cues should be in tune with these expressions of need.

When essential needs *are* met, and met with adequate consistency, an infant learns to expect that what is needed will continue to be provided by the mother or mother-substitute. It is this consistency which forms the basis for security, and for a developing expectation that good experience will be repeated and that bad experience will continue to be dealt with. It is on this basis that an infant begins to be hopeful, even if only pre-consciously.

In this context I find it helpful to use the distinction described in Chapter 6, between needs and (libidinal) demands or wants. As development proceeds we can see that the needs I shall be speaking of are not necessarily synonymous with libido. Here I am considering, in more detail, needs that are fundamental to growth which I think of as growth-needs.

To begin with, therefore, I am using unconscious hope to include any form of striving towards what is needed. When it is something as basic as food that is searched for we can speak of instinct. When an older child shows signs of needing fresh adaptation (in others) to changing needs, it is not so easy to explain the unconscious sureness with which this seems to be sought out or indicated. What is needed, at times of transition into a new phase of development, has not yet been experienced – and yet it is indicated by means of unconscious cues to parents or to the care-giving world. We can also see much evidence of this in our clinical work.

Let me give an example to illustrate some of what I have been saying so far. Bion considers a hypothetical first feed, and suggests that the infant has a preconception of a breast before the breast is first encountered (Bion 1967b: 111–12). Winnicott, somewhat similarly, suggests that the infant (out of experienced need) 'creates' an illusion of a breast (Winnicott 1958: 238–9; 1988: 100–5). When the mother places her actual breast within reach of the infant we notice the familiar rooting for the nipple, finding it, and eventually suckling. We can then postulate that the infant has found what it had been looking for, even though suckling at a breast had never been experienced before. Subsequently, because of that first feed, we can interpret the infant's repeated search for the breast (when hungry) as based increasingly upon experience.

Now, if we think of this sequence in terms of unconscious hope we could say the mother recognizes that her infant's first rooting for the nipple indicates an expectation of finding it. Later, based upon repeated experience, the infant may develop a sense of hope that what is needed can again be looked for and found: hope here lies in the infant's capacity to offer cues which is reinforced by another person's capacity to respond to them.

Needing and wanting

One could say that needing and wanting are synonymous during most of the first year of life. And yet there are signs of some distinction between them even in the new-born. For instance, when an infant is giving clear indications of hunger it does not always follow that the breast is immediately accepted when presented. The hunger (wanting food) is still evident; but sometimes there is also a recognizable need for something else. It may be, as Winnicott has suggested, that the infant needs 'a period of hesitation' in which to rediscover the breast; or it may be that the breast has been invested by the infant with persecutory qualities, due to a prolonged delay in being available, or in being too quickly presented for feeding. The infant then needs the mother to understand this reluctance to feed, or to have an intuitive patience whilst her baby rediscovers a good breast, as it were 'beyond' that which may have been experienced as bad and to be avoided. Through the mother's tolerance of this period of hesitation, the infant is better able to rediscover the breast subsequently as a good object, again able to nourish.

What makes the problem more difficult to resolve is when a mother is too anxious to see herself as a good object to her hungry infant. This can result in premature attempts at feeding. The offered breast may then be experienced as an impingement, fitting into a phantasy of the breast as an attacking object. The infant's need to be allowed time to rediscover the breast as a good object may be overlooked because the infant is also showing signs of wanting to be fed.

Sometimes there is a similar problem between the patient and analyst, often due to an experience which has led the patient to perceive the analyst as persecutory. This can dovetail with a need to use the analyst as a bad object, representing some past bad experience which has become dynamically present in the transference. There is then a need to work through unresolved feelings towards the earlier object-relationship that is now represented in this so-called 'negative transference'. (Incidentally, I question the unqualified description of this as 'negative' because some very positive results are frequently achieved through working with this form of transference.)

The patient's unconscious hope here is, in my opinion, that the analyst will be better able to tolerate this use of him in the transference than the original object(s) had been. If this is the case, important steps can be achieved towards recovery from past traumatic experience. The patient may press the analyst to demonstrate his presence as a good object in order to ward off the bad experience that is being relived in the transference. But this is not in the patient's best interest. The wanting and the needing here are quite contrary (see Chapter 5; also Casement 1985: ch. 7).

Unconscious hope expressed in child development

I find it interesting that at each stage of development we can see some evidence of what I am calling unconscious hope in a child's behaviour which could alert the mother (or parents) that there is some fresh growth-need to be attended to. And it is then that we also see evidence of a growing distinction between needing and wanting. But, in each case, someone has to recognize behaviour as a cue for what is needed. For instance:

(i) The more mobile child begins to get into everything, wanting to explore and to gratify a widening curiosity about the world around. The fresh need then is for a greater alertness to the infant's safety. And, when this is lacking, behaviour often follows that expresses the unmet need ever more clearly.

(ii) A child who is beginning to negotiate the difficult problem of facing even manageable degrees of frustration will often have tantrums. And when a child is in a tantrum it is all too apparent that it is wanting something, desperately wanting it – even if it is only in order to have its own way. But what the child is also needing is something very different. The unconscious hope here, I would suggest, is for someone to provide a parental firmness that can help the child to cope with frustration that is age-appropriate. This firmness can only be effectively provided by a parent who has the confidence to bear the rage which may often follow when limits are set upon the child's demands (Casement 1969).

I believe that we could think of the sequence here as indicating an unconscious search for a framework that can provide a child with a much needed security. Without this the child develops a sense of an unstoppable rage within. This can only become tamed when it is experienced as manageable by another. If that containment by another person continues to be lacking, I do not think that the hope I am speaking of necessarily ceases to exist. The child continues to present parents (or others) with behaviour that demonstrates the search for what is needed.

(iii) If a child finds one parent easy to get round, compared with the other who is trying to set limits, it is likely to take advantage of that split. But this is always a hollow triumph. Often, therefore, a child will press ever more noticeably for further gratification from the permissive parent, to a point where this may bring about more open discord between the parents over their different handling of the child. I think that we could see this as expressing an unconscious hope that such parents will eventually begin to see a need to get together on the issue of limit-setting. The child's need for containment may then begin to be attended to.

A brief example, taken from my work with Joy (Chapter 3), will illustrate what I am saying.

Example 7.1

Joy had been behaving in ways that clearly indicated a *need for firmness* in handling her anger, which she had previously not been able to find. Her mother seemed to have indulged her when Joy was angry with her; her father had often been absent. Consequently, when Joy was with me, she would sometimes become almost uncontrollable – to the point where I had to be very firm in preventing her from scratching, kicking or biting, when she was angry with me for not letting her have her own way. Without my firmness she seemed to be quite unable to control herself.

I eventually had to hold Joy's wrists to control her, whilst she shouted: 'Let go, let go!' (see Session 21). *I had to control her with my holding of her until she was ready to hold herself.*

Several times we went through a similar sequence, with the same kind of shift from destructive behaviour to something positive. I believe that her difficult behaviour had been expressing an unconscious hope that she might eventually find the holding that she needed, from someone able to survive her rages. Only thus was she able to experience herself as controllable, at first by someone else then by herself.

In the analytic encounter, in different ways, we are presented with similar needs for firmness. We meet these differently, without having to provide a physical holding; but we still have to meet this challenge if the patient is going to feel securely held in the analytic relationship.

Unconscious hope in the 'antisocial tendency'

Unconscious hope is quite specifically expressed in pre-delinquent behaviour, which Winnicott calls 'the antisocial tendency'. He says of this: '[It] *is not a diagnosis*. It does not compare directly with other diagnostic terms such as neurosis and psychosis. The antisocial tendency may be found in a normal individual, or in one that is neurotic or psychotic' (Winnicott 1958: 308). Later, he says: 'The treatment of the antisocial tendency is not psychoanalysis but management, a going to meet and match the moment of hope' (Winnicott 1958: 309).

Older children, when their parents fail to respond to their prompting for them to be better parents, often extend the unconscious search for what is missing by behaving towards other parental figures in similar ways. Teachers, and sometimes the police, are then prompted to provide a firmness that has not yet been found within the family. But it is a caring firmness that is being looked for; and when that is still not forthcoming, the consequent antisocial behaviour may become more truly delinquent. I believe that this shift into delinquency, when it occurs, is often motivated by a sense of let-down that follows from the unconscious hope for containment (or understanding) not having been met. Subsequently, the secondary gains from delinquency may eventually mask, even obliterate, the original search that had remained unfulfilled. But I do not think the hope then ceases to exist; instead it enters the repressed unconscious, and becomes evident through more oblique derivative communication.

When a child has been deprived of some necessary provision, and has missed this for longer than can be managed by internal resources alone, the child may sometimes go in search of what is missing – symbolically – through stealing – *when hopeful* (Winnicott 1958: 310).

> Example 7.2
>
> When I was a probation officer, I came to see the parents of a ten-year-old girl (Mary) who had been picked up for shop-lifting. I was told that this child had taken a number of objects, from several different shops, before she was noticed. The police had been called and she was taken to her home, whereupon her father had been called in to be present whilst she was being questioned. Her father, I discovered, was a policeman.

Thinking about this now, we can readily imagine some of what Mary may have wanted. She may have felt that she wanted what she had stolen; she may have wanted to punish her father for spending time more readily with her two older brothers than with her; and she may have unconsciously wished him to be a policeman to her, an externalized superego. *But what Mary needed was a father who could also be a father to her.* It was therefore important to help this couple recognize her unmet need, particularly as the father's first response had been to lose his temper and to shout: 'I never thought that we would have a thief in our own family.'

It was, of course, necessary to work with this family for some time for Mary's need to be convincingly met. Fortunately, the father was later able to see that he had been showing preferential treatment to the boys, and he began to find time in which Mary could also be special to him. So, she found what she had been unconsciously looking for – and she did not need to steal again.

In this example, the unconscious hope (a search for a father for herself) was not disappointed. Sometimes, however, such pre-delinquent behaviour is not recognized for what it is – an unconscious search for something missing – and the moment of hope is wasted (Winnicott 1958: 309).

Other manifestations of unconscious hope

It can be a useful exercise to think of some examples of behaviour difficulty, in child development or later, and to wonder about these in order to distinguish what the different elements of

unconscious communication may have been in each. For
instance:

(i) In the familiar phenomenon of an older child's bed-wetting
when a new baby is born, we can readily recognize a wish for
mother's attention, and probably also a wish to be allowed to be
the baby again. Equally we can imagine unconscious phantasies,
wishing to attack the mother with urine and probably the baby
too; or we may postulate a wish to create a substitute warmth in
this experience of wetting, perhaps to replace the mother's
warmth, and so on. But if we think more specifically of what is
needed here by the older child we may be able to discern an
element also of unconscious hope: a hope that the mother might
understand and attend to her older child's jealousy and distress.
If the mother is then able to respond sensitively to that need, it
often happens that the bed-wetting (as a communication that has
achieved its aim) may begin to be less frequent, until it stops.

(ii) If we think of the seductive behaviour of an Oedipal child we
can readily see a wish to get some special attention from the
opposite-sex parent. We can also imagine various unconscious
phantasies to do with getting rid of the rival parent and an
unconscious wish to replace him/her. But it is also useful to
consider what the unconscious hope may be. The growth-need is
for the child's budding sexuality to be affirmed: not to be
ignored, run away from, or exploited.

Unconscious hope in the clinical setting

When there has been some degree of failure in meeting the
growth-needs, we are likely to find these re-presented in the
clinical setting.

For instance, when there has been some failure in meeting the
needs of Oedipal development, it is important that the unconscious hope should be recognized as it comes to be expressed in
the analytic relationship. Typically, a patient may demonstrate a
continuing need for sexuality to be affirmed – to be treated as a
positive force in the patient, not as bad or overwhelmingly
strong, nor as non-existent. It is therefore important that analysts
can interpret a patient's sexuality, when this becomes evident
within the analytic relationship, in ways that indicate an
awareness of the unmet needs. It is not helpful to interpret
evidence of a patient's sexuality in the session merely as being
seductive – as if this were bad or as if the patient should not be

expressing this sexuality towards the analyst. It is often more productive if such behaviour can be understood in terms of a search for affirmation and containment. And, once again, it is essential that we do not confuse needing with wanting here. The patient might want to seduce the analyst; but the unconscious need and hope will be to find an analyst who is not afraid of this seductiveness, and who is able to contain it by understanding why this behaviour is being presented in the analysis by the patient.

I now wish to give some brief references to the various ways in which I think that patients contribute hopefully towards finding the clinical setting that is needed. And I find it uncanny, sometimes, that patients who have had no experience of analysis or psychotherapy nevertheless seem to have a sense of what is necessary for them to progress therapeutically. I felt this most particularly during my work with Joy (Chapter 3).

For example, when a patient is using previous changes in arrangements as a basis for expecting further exceptions, this may also be a tacit prompt for more firmness in these arrangements: frequently, we will discover that a caring firmness had been absent in childhood. Similarly, any deviation by the analyst from the usual professional boundaries is often taken advantage of – the patient wanting more; but this too may be an unconscious cue that the analytic boundaries need to be more clearly established and maintained. Sometimes, I believe, we can see both a wish to exploit a weakness in the professional setting and a hope that the issues pointed to in this way will be better attended to. These unconscious prompts are, I think, essentially hopeful.

The unconscious search for new solutions

In repetition compulsion

A typical expression of unconscious hope may be found in repetition compulsion, when unresolved conflicts continue to generate attempts at solutions which do not really work. Once a genuine solution is found then the compulsion to repeat will usually diminish and eventually stop.

In role-responsiveness

When analysts allow themselves to be responsive to their patients' unconscious cues, they will be prompted into becoming different with each patient (Sandler 1976; 1983). What can follow from this responsiveness is sometimes strangely specific to the patient's life experience. Occasionally, the analyst may find himself being prodded into behaving in some way that is similar to a significant person who had let the patient down in earlier life. He will then be used to represent an element of parental failure from the past, becoming the object of whatever feelings had been associated with that earlier failure (see Chapters 5 and 6). It is thus within the immediacy of this experience in the transference relationship, that the patient has a further opportunity to work through feelings that had been unmanageable in the past and therefore repressed.

Example 7.3

I was once seeing a patient in twice-a-week psychotherapy. (I will call him David.) His sessions had originally been on Mondays and Thursdays, but the gap between these had become an obstacle to continuity in the therapy. As David was not able to come more frequently I had suggested that he might come on consecutive days, and this had resulted in a quite new shift in his therapy. He was able to use the first of each pair of sessions more freely because of there being a session on the following day; and the bigger gap in the week was less of a problem than might have been expected.

It so happened that David is a twin. He and his brother had been breast fed until they were about three months old. Then the mother had become suddenly ill and had to be admitted to hospital. The twins went too but had to be fed by a number of different nurses, the mother being unable to attend to them for about three days. Upon her recovery it was found that breast feeding could not be re-established. The 'older' twin would then not allow anyone else but the mother to attend to him. David, however, had become compliant – allowing himself to be fed by anyone available. This compliance was not recognized as a signal of his distress but had been mistaken for contentment.

About six months after the sessions had been established on consecutive days, I was having difficulty in finding a time for a new analytic patient. I am sure that it was no accident that I first thought of asking my most obliging patient (David) to change one session to another day, with one day between sessions, and he readily agreed. However, the next week (for the first time since I had started seeing him) David came to a session two minutes late. Before that he had always been either early or exactly on time.

When I thought about this quite unusual lateness, and the silence with which he began the session, I began to realize that this was a whispered protest against the change in days – probably representing a rage that David did not feel able to express more directly. Fortunately, I was able to recognize this protest and to attend to it. I was able to let him keep to his usual session-times instead of persisting with my request for this further change.

What followed then was David becoming able to be more forceful, with a fresh belief that protest could be heard. And, as part of that new protesting, I was soon to be subjected to the feelings of rage that originally belonged to the mother, who (like me) had exploited this twin's readiness to fit in with what was expected of him.

In this experience with me, David was able to have attention given to his very early need. His mother had not recognized his distress beneath the defence of compliance; she was therefore not able to attend to that distress. But I believe there had remained an unconscious hope that, in some way, the unmet needs (which remained concealed beneath his compliance but were also indicated by it) could one day be recognized and be met. And that repeating pattern of compliance, so often exploited by others, had been an expression of that continued striving for attention to be given to the distress that had been overlooked before.

It is here too that an essential and therapeutic difference can be discovered by the patient, in that the analyst is able to recover from an element of his own failure in the analytic relationship. But that recovery cannot occur unless the analyst is willing to respond to the patient's corrective cues: it is this readiness to rethink, when things have gone wrong, that has often been missing in the patient's past relationships – particularly when parents had too often believed that they were in the right.

In this unconscious role-responsiveness we find something of what Winnicott had been referring to when he wrote of the patient 'using the analyst's failures' (Winnicott 1958: ch. 22; 1965: ch. 23), and here he invokes a notion very close to that of unconscious hope. In another passage he writes of a defence against specific environmental failure by a *freezing of the failure situation*.

> Along with this [freezing] goes an unconscious assumption (which can become a conscious hope) that opportunity will

occur at a later date for a renewed experience in which the
failure situation will be able to be unfrozen and
re-experienced, with the individual in a regressed state, in an
environment that is making adequate adaptation.

(Winnicott 1958: 281)

The patient uses the analyst's failure in the here-and-now to
represent past failures in parental care. And when the analytic
relationship feels secure enough, the patient rages against the
analyst and so acts upon his feelings more fully than had been
possible in relation to the original mother or mother-substitute,
who had failed the patient in ways now being re-enacted in the
transference relationship. This is very different from any question
of trying to be the better parent. If anything better *is* to be found
in this, it grows out of the analyst's capacity to tolerate the
feelings which come to be directed at him/her, when the analyst is
used to represent the earlier *bad* experience. The original
parent(s) had usually been unable to deal with those feelings –
even if only because they could not be spoken about. (Often, an
important factor of early trauma had been that it could not be put
into words.)

In projective identification

Another powerful way in which unconscious hope may be
expressed clinically is through projective identification – when
patients seek to get rid of, into the analyst, aspects of the self (or
states of feeling) that cannot be managed alone. The unconscious
hope here is that the analyst will be able to manage that which is
being projected into him/her which patients cannot manage in
themselves without help.

When projective identification is understood in this way it is
clear why it is so important that analysts should be able to
manage within themselves whatever is being 'put into' them, and
to do so with a sensitivity to the patient's need to seek help in this
way.

The projection of hope and despair

An important example of communication by means of projective
identification is encountered when a patient presents in a state of
despair. Superficially, it might look as if despair were the
ultimate negation of hope. But I believe that we can see evidence
of unconscious hope here in two forms.

More commonly recognized is the projection of a patient's hope into the analyst, the patient not being able to preserve that hope alongside the experience of despair. At such a moment we might say that the analyst has to carry the hope for the patient until such time as it can be accepted by the patient as his/her own. A common response, outside of analysis and psychotherapy, is to try reassuring the despairing person with sayings such as: 'There will be light at the end of the tunnel.' A more analytical response would be to say something like: 'While you are feeling so much despair, I think you are needing me to hold on to the hope that you cannot feel in yourself just now.'

Though that interpretation may be adequate (as far as it goes) it is likely to leave the patient still alone with the despair. If the other person can only feel the patient's projected hope, and not the despair, it could seem as if that despair cannot be tolerated. I have often noticed how important it is for a despairing patient to be able to communicate the despair directly – so that the analyst or therapist feels it too. What is then received by the analyst is the patient's own intolerable experience, and the patient is no longer so alone with it. This suggests that the analyst should be capable of a benign split within himself; being able to take in and experience the patient's despair, and yet being able still to see the possibility of not having to give up under the weight of it (see *example 5.7*).

The nature of unconscious hope here is subtle and important. Obviously, the patient is not conscious of the hope that is projected into the analyst. Also, when hope gives way to despair it becomes repressed. I wish to suggest that it is this unconscious and repressed hope that now shows itself in the form of despair. The unmet need is then for someone else to be available to the patient, with the capacity to be truly in touch with what the patient is feeling until things feel better. Often, in the patient's past, there has been a traumatic absence of this emotional holding. It is then in the analytic relationship that it will again be searched for.

Threats of suicide

I believe that, almost always, when a person talks of suicide there is a double message. One part of this is saying that life (as it is) has become unbearable; the other part is appealing for someone to be available to help change it. There may be an element of unconscious hope even in threats of suicide. It is therefore important that there is someone available to respond to such a plea, however deeply it may be hidden, in order to do whatever can be done towards changing what can be changed. One change could be that someone is prepared to be in touch with the unbearable state of suicidal desperation. It is therefore a most dangerous, even though popular, assumption that the person who speaks about suicide will not die of suicide. This view just encourages people to become unresponsive to the unconscious hope that may be in the suicide's plea for some form of help that has not yet been forthcoming. If no one responds to that remaining element of hope, then a successful attempt at suicide may follow – a final act of despair and retaliation against a world seen as uncaring.

The communication of hurt

I believe that we can sometimes see evidence of unconscious hope in hurtful behaviour. A hurt child will often behave hurtfully to others, identifying with some past or recent aggressor and attempting to pass on to others the hurt received. The unconscious hope here may simply be to get rid of that hurt: sometimes, however, it may be to receive help with it. When the unconscious meaning of hurtful behaviour is understood in this way, it becomes easier to attend to the child's experience of hurt, and the behaviour does not have to be regarded simply as bad – let alone as sadistic. However, when the needed attention to the hurt is not forthcoming, the earlier search for help may give way to the secondary gains of some pleasure discovered in hurting. This, I believe, is a contributory factor in the aetiology of sadism that is often overlooked. When the unconscious hope in hurtful behaviour is disappointed it may be repressed, and subsequently be in evidence only through the unconscious derivative of sadistic behaviour. When this becomes sexualized, it is yet further removed from the unconscious hope that may initially have been expressed in such behaviour. As with delinquency, when the needs that are indicated in hurtful behaviour continue to be unmet, there is a tendency to retaliate against those who have failed to meet that need. The hurt child then punishes those who fail him/her and the attachment to the secondary gains in sadistic behaviour may become addictive.

Conclusion

I would like to summarize the factors that I believe to indicate the presence of unconscious hope. There is usually some problematic behaviour (or attitude) that attracts the attention of others; the behaviour is usually non-satisfying in terms of what is really needed; it frequently becomes more noticeable, and often more difficult for others to manage, until what is needed is recognized and appropriately responded to. When this form of communication is interpreted in terms of that unconscious search, or as evidence of some unconscious hope of finding what is needed, patients often indicate a sense of having been understood – and what is unconsciously being looked for may begin to be found.

Finally, I wish to stress that at no time is unconscious hope more vital than when a patient is putting an analyst through the roughest of times. Even though treatment may intermittently look totally hopeless, and the analyst may be made to feel entirely hopeless too, it is most important not to lose sight of the fact that such problems in treatment are often (in themselves) an expression of the patient's unconscious search for some help – never previously found – with serious emotional difficulties. What the patient needs is to find someone who can bear being really in touch with the patient's extremes of personal difficulty without having to give up, someone who (without being unrealistic or trying to be omnipotent) can find some way to see the patient through. If an analyst begins to feel convinced that this will not be possible, I believe that it is then essential that he/she should seek whatever outside help may be necessary in order not to reject a patient: often the problem in the analytic relationship crucially represents precisely what is needing to be worked at in the analysis. Therefore, if an analysis is not to be prematurely terminated, becoming able to see the patient through may involve the analyst in seeking consultation (at the very least) or on-going supervision for a time (perhaps). Occasionally, a similar impasse with several patients may indicate a need for further personal analysis (for the analyst) if patients are not going to be subjected to a repetition, in the analytic treatment, of earlier failures by others. But when an analyst is able to find the capacity to see a patient through such extremely difficult times, ultimately the unconscious hope is met.[3]

Chapter eight

Inner and outer realities[1]

Which realities do we find in the analytic encounter? There seems always to be an intermingling of the objective and the subjective realities of each participant – an intermingling of how each sees the other as well as how each may believe him/herself to be. Inevitably, therefore, the analyst's ways of being with the patient will affect what passes between them – as will the impact of the patient upon the analyst. These interactive pressures can disturb the analytic process or become part of it, depending upon whether they are recognized and how they are understood.

Introduction

It is common knowledge amongst the psychoanalytically minded, but not so well known to others, that in all relationships the other person is seen in terms of the internal world of the perceiver.

In this chapter, I wish to consider various ways in which the external and internal realities of analyst and patient affect each other, and how these in turn can either disturb the analytic process or become an integral part of it. I also wish to illustrate ways in which patients can use the objective realities of the analytic relationship to represent aspects of their own internal world, and those experiences that still need to be worked through.

The environment and the inner world

The present is often viewed so determinedly in terms of past experience that it takes a lot of careful work before the present can be seen for itself – as separate and different from the past. In the course of that work we frequently find evidence of early

125

environmental failure etched into the patient's internal world, which in turn affects how subsequent experience is viewed and related to.

Example 8.1

Some time ago a man (Mr L) came to see me, saying that he needed help to change his life. Then, to explain this, he added: 'You see, I suffered a severe environmental set-back in my infancy.' What he was trying to tell me was that his mother had died before he was two.

As well as telling me this detail of his early life, Mr L was demonstrating a number of other important facts about himself. His stilted way of talking reflected his experience of institutionalized life: he had spent most of his childhood in care. It also illustrated how far removed he had become from the emotional impact of his mother's death, which had remained beyond words – at least beyond those that had any warmth or emotional significance for him.

There was little or no warmth in his inner world. He had no conscious memory of his mother. So he had no available sense of an internal mother from whom to derive warmth or inner security. Instead, in this man's inner world there remained an absent mother; or, to be more precise, he had a repressed memory of a caring presence that had suddenly been replaced by an absence. An indelible link had thus come to be established in this man's mind between a warm presence and traumatic loss; as if death, or some other rejection, would inevitably follow any good experience with another person. As a result he had come to expect everybody to let him down in one way or another. Any possibility of warmth in a relationship had been shunned throughout his life, because he regarded this as a warning sign that he would again be hurt if he dared to expect it to continue.

So, we find here a common pattern: the nature of inner reality is largely based upon early experience and is little affected for the better by subsequent changes in the external world. Mr L's early experience of loss had come to colour his perception of all subsequent relationships. As a result, caring relationships, although desperately needed, had come to be feared and fiercely avoided.

I referred this patient to a female colleague, who later told me of his problems in that analysis. In particular, it had been difficult for her to find an appropriate balance in her technique. On the one hand, Mr L had experienced her more usual stance of clinical distance as confirming his view of the world as anonymous and uncaring; and yet, because it was familiar, that felt 'safe' to him. On the other hand, when Mr L sensed a genuine caring in his analyst, he experienced that warmth as a danger-signal because of the link in his mind between warmth and loss. Much analytic work had therefore been necessary in order to build a bridge between the reality of the patient's inner world and a different reality in which caring did not necessarily have to lead to rejection or loss.

The inner world realized

I will now give some details from part of an analysis in which I had to find my own way of dealing with a similar conflict, between a patient's need to find security in a dependent relationship and her experience of dependence as dangerous.

Example 8.2

Miss M was the only child of her unmarried mother. She came to me for analysis when she was twenty-two. Having been brought up in Europe she had come to this country to escape from what she had felt to be the grip of a possessive and cruel mother.

Miss M described her mother as if she only felt hated by her. From an early age she had, apparently, been treated as her mother's slave. From about four years old she had been expected to wash up and clean, and from the age of ten she had to do much of the cooking after school whilst her mother was still at work. But whatever Miss M did, her mother would invariably find fault: she seemed to be totally unpleasable.

Miss M's mother, I was told, used also to respond with sarcasm, denigration or abuse, to any emotional needs expressed by her daughter. There seemed to be one sacred rule – that she should never disturb her mother in any way. So, from very early on, if Miss M ever expressed distress to her mother she was fobbed off with various tranquillizers. Any expectation that her mother should attend to her (except for giving pills) was immediately attacked as being 'selfish'.

Rather inevitably, Miss M had learned not to turn to people but to substitutes. Initially she turned to food for comfort. Then, during her last year at school, she had become addicted to drugs. A few years later she nearly died after an unintended over-dose, which so frightened her she developed a phobia against drugs and against almost any kind of medication. Subsequently, she turned to cigarettes and drink as alternative ways of trying to banish difficult feelings, and she was well on her way to becoming an alcoholic when she first came to me. Her reason for seeking analysis was that she felt she was in danger of going mad.

In the early stages of seeing Miss M, I was given many details of her life – but it was noticeable that she barely related to me as a person. I might sometimes be told of difficult situations, or of difficult feelings, but I was not expected to be of any help with either. Her inner reality cautioned her that, under no circumstances, was any person to be trusted or to be turned to because of need.

One defence used by Miss M was that of creating splits in herself. She saw herself as having several distinct selves, one that was public and seemingly self-sufficient and another that was very needy but carefully hidden. Another version of this split was to be found in her illusion of never being alone: she always had a pretend companion – and sometimes she had voices. She felt that she kept herself 'sane' by having conversations between her different selves. Between them they could safely criticize her mother, and could mock at people who needed people: her different selves had each other and therefore needed nobody. She eventually told me that one of her voices had been constantly deriding me, throughout the first years of her analysis, for thinking that she might eventually let me help her.

In the transference I was sometimes the person whom she needed to be a mother to her; but, at the same time, I represented her actual mother in relation to whom she had to demonstrate that she had no needs. So, when I tried to interpret her real need of me, and most particularly when I expressed the view that she needed me as a mother to her, she either scorned me for my stupidity or she became terrified that I was threatening to *become* her mother. 'What is the matter with you?' she said. 'Are you trying to drive me crazy?'

A major problem here, I had to realize, was that my use of the word 'mother' had nothing but frightening associations for Miss M. In her experience, a mother had been someone who attacked her for being needy. The person whom she still needed to find was someone who could be different from her mother and who could really take care of her. She had no word for this, but that person was certainly not thought of as a mother. It was therefore a long time before Miss M could discover that a mother could also be someone who attends to the needs of her child.

The patient's criticisms of me became increasingly fierce and sarcastic. Whatever I said was disagreed with. Every interpretation was challenged and mockingly treated as wrong. She began withdrawing into silence, often hiding under a blanket on the couch, or she would sullenly chain smoke throughout a session.[2] She didn't need me, and she had her conversations – so why should she speak to me? And yet she never failed to attend for her analysis.

Gradually it dawned upon me how the transference had shifted. The patient was 'identifying with the aggressor'; and I was now being used to represent herself as the victim whom she attacked with her mother's derision. Like herself as a child, I was now regarded as failing to get anything right.

When I first tried to interpret this view of what was happening I failed to anticipate that Miss M was more likely to respond to the form of my interpretation than to its content. I had said to her: 'You are now treating me as your mother treated you.' She reacted immediately to the implied criticism in my use of the word 'now', as if I were adding yet another complaint to other complaints. She said, scornfully: 'If you can't stand it then you shouldn't be pretending to me that you can help me.'

Sometime later I tried a different approach. I said to her: 'I believe that you are communicating to me something very important. I believe that you are unconsciously trying to get across to me *what it was like to be you in the presence of your mother*; so that I can now have a clear sense of the frustration and pain that you endured as a result of her always finding fault with you, and of her scorn and criticism. I think that this is why you have needed to treat me in ways similar to how your mother treated you.' This time Miss M was unusually reflective. She eventually replied: 'I think that you are beginning to understand.'

That session proved to be a turning point in this difficult, but eventually productive, analysis. The essential difference (this time) was that I had been more careful to create an atmosphere of understanding, in which the patient's behaviour could be seen as a communication, and accepted, before trying once again to look at that behaviour which the patient expected me to criticize.

I believe that Miss M had needed to re-create a central feature of her mother's treatment of her within the relationship to me. Her inner reality thus came to be *actualized* within the analysis (Sandler 1976), whereby she made real to me that experience of her mother – at least as she had herself experienced it. (See also King 1978.)

Here, as with any patient, we have to face a further problem in deciding which reality we are dealing with. Miss M could give me only her own account of *her experience with her mother*, and that would inevitably be deeply coloured by her feelings and phantasies towards her. So, as well as the mother's real cruelty (which seemed to be verified independently by other people's views of her), I had to consider the possibility of the patient's own attacking that might have been projected on to the mother. But that too was complex, as I could sense a vicious circle in which any attacking that may have been projected by the patient would have been reinforced by the attacking behaviour of her mother. It was therefore not possible to be sure, at any given moment, which was primary. But, on balance, I felt that the mother's inability to respond to her daughter's appeals to her, to be a mother, remained consistent and central to the clinical picture. In addition, it is quite likely that Miss M used to project *into* her mother the unmanageable rage and distress that she could not cope with alone. The result then would probably have been that the patient's rage and distress were experienced as repeatedly 'thrown back' at her, made worse by the fact that the mother was also unable to manage these things in herself – let alone take on what her daughter could not manage (Bion 1967b: 114–16).

In the patient's internal world, then, there was certainly a persecutory mother. There was also a split between the patient's needy self and her self-as-companion upon whom alone she felt that she could depend. This split had been developed very early through her discovery that the only attention she could expect to find for her needs was that which she provided for herself. And it is significant that Miss M's own word here was 'companion' (someone friendly who stayed with her). It was a long time before she could tolerate any link between this and my notion of her need for a mother's care and holding.

What eventually began to shift this defensive self-sufficiency was the patient's discovery that I could understand and tolerate her use of me as the object of her attacks. From that discovery she was able to recognize that I could bear to remain in touch with her own most painful experiences, which was precisely what her mother could not bear being expected to help her with.

Then, from that earlier self-sufficiency and dependence upon substances rather than upon people, Miss M began to allow herself to depend upon me in the analysis. These changes in the transference relationship reflected changes that had occurred within her internal world. She had now discovered a different reality, based upon her objective experience of me, in which it began to feel safe for her to relate to people and to risk becoming dependent – at first upon me and subsequently upon the man who later became her husband. The word 'mother', too, ceased to be synonymous with cruelty; and, some years later, Miss M was able to become a sensitive and imaginative mother to her own child.

The analyst's environmental provision

Implicit in this second example was the need for the patient to discover that she was in the presence of someone whose underlying attitude to her sustained a wish to understand her behaviour rather than to criticize it. But she could not believe *that* so long as my way of interpreting really did sound critical to her. It had then not been enough for me merely to suggest that Miss M was experiencing me as her critical mother and therefore reading criticism into what I was saying. That interpretation had been dismissed by her as *my refusal to consider the truth of what she was saying*. But, by trial-identifying with the patient, I could more readily recognize an implied criticism in what I had said and I could see the need for me to find other ways of interpreting to her that were more clearly neutral.

It is, therefore, important to remember that some patients are acutely sensitive to the hidden meanings in what the analyst says. And I believe that it is harmful to the analytic process when analysts appear to ignore a patient's accurate perception, or interpret defensively in the face of it.

The analyst's style of working

There are certain clinical states that are especially affected by the analyst's style of interpreting. I am thinking of compliant or false-self states, in patients who have adapted to a regime of parental impingements by taking over their parents' definition of what is real. I am also thinking of patients who have suffered narcissistic injury, having been made to feel bad about themselves in relation to their primary object(s).

With patients who are suffering from compliant or false-self states, much will depend upon whether the analyst behaves in an impinging way or allows adequate space for the patient to risk being more real. Too much interpretation, or interpretation that is given in a dogmatic way, is likely to invite further compliance.

What is more helpful with such patients is a more tentative style of interpreting and an analytic presence that is less obtrusive (Balint 1968: ch. 25).

In relation to narcissistic injury, much will rest upon whether the analyst remains sufficiently sensitive to the patient's underlying vulnerability, and avoids becoming too intent upon eliminating the symptomatic behaviour. Pathology serves a communicative as well as a defensive function (see Chapter 7). This is sometimes overlooked when an analyst is confronted by narcissistic defences: for, when these defences are aimed at protecting the vulnerable self, they are frequently destructive of the capacity for object relating.

If narcissistic pathology is interpreted too insistently as due to an innate destructiveness in the patient, rather than understood as a defence against unbearable anxieties, an analyst can fall into an attitude towards a patient that is more critical than understanding. What then follows can amount to a battle between an attacking analyst and a patient whose defensive posture may largely be a response to the analyst. It is all too easy to fall into such an interaction, particularly if the analyst fails to recognize his/her own part in this, and it can further develop into a transference-countertransference enactment that has its roots in the history of both combatants. The analyst will then urgently need to recover a more neutral stance from which to reflect upon such moments as these.

The wounding interpretations that narcissistically vulnerable patients sometimes attract, based on the analyst's desire to break through the narcissistic shell, can also become a re-enactment of an original trauma. Such re-enactments may therefore have diagnostic significance, pointing to a similar breakdown of early parental containment.

Another feature with narcissistically damaged patients is that, whilst conscious guilt may apparently be absent, the patient's unconscious guilt is often already extreme and unbearable.[3] This can lead to a form of interpretive work that, in itself, becomes persecutory, particularly if the compliant patient finds a superego role-responsiveness in the analyst. Unfortunately, patients may then show changes in symptomatology which are brought about by virtue of a strengthening of the already harsh superego, or an intensification of splitting. Furthermore, a sado-masochistic relationship can develop which is not always recognized as such by either patient or analyst.

Reality and impasse in the analysis

There are some occasions when an analysis begins to fail, or fails completely, because an impasse has developed between analyst and patient.[4] Often this has resulted from a loss of the analytic space, which can easily happen if the analyst has *in objective reality* become too much like a key figure in the patient's internal world. When that happens the analysis cannot continue effectively until a sufficient difference has again been established between the analyst and the particular transference use of the analyst by the patient (see Chapter 5). If the analyst denies his or her contribution to this similarity, that adds a pathogenic dimension to the analytic relationship, which then makes it quite unanalysable until the objective reality has been attended to by the analyst (see *example 7.3*). Some analysts have a problem about admitting their mistakes which, they fear, might be personally revealing or might seem to involve some loss of face. My impression, however, is that patients ultimately feel more secure (not less) when they discover that the analyst can acknowledge and learn from mistakes.

Therapeutic use of re-enactment

Re-enactment by the analyst, if it is not understood and remedied, is always likely to disturb the analytic process. Sometimes, however, this re-enactment seems to evolve from the analytic process itself. I am thinking of those occasions when an uncanny parallel to a key experience in the patient's life develops around some real event involving the analyst. This then takes on a double significance. At one level it becomes a trigger for transference; at another it involves the analyst in a way that enables the patient to feel justified in expressing towards the analyst, in the present, feelings that belonged originally to some earlier bad experience.

Finally, therefore, I wish to give a brief example to show how a patient's inner reality can sometimes be stumbled upon in this way.

Example 8.3

Mrs P, as I shall call her, was in her early thirties when she came into analysis with me.

In her second year she came into a session in a state of great agitation. She demanded to know why I had allowed the patient before her to come back into the waiting-room whilst she was there. (He had, in fact, left a briefcase there and had gone back to fetch it.)

A few weeks later that man did the same thing again. Mrs P then became utterly enraged, and she expressed her views on this very forcefully: I should have been more watchful; I should have seen what he was up to; I should have made sure that he would never do that again; how could I have let it go on happening? And what kind of analyst did I think I was, allowing that to have happened at all let alone more than once? This incident became the focus for weeks of angry protesting and distrust. It was clear that the patient regarded me as careless, perhaps even as not caring. But the intensity of Mrs P's distress suggested that there was something more in this that we did not yet understand.

A dream then helped to clarify what this sequence had come to represent. In this dream Mrs P was in her parents' home. She was quite small. The man from my waiting-room had come into where she was, in her bedroom. She had started screaming for her mother but nobody came. She had woken up in a state of terror.

Mrs P was very disturbed after dreaming this. It brought back vivid memories. It reminded her of the man who lived next door to her childhood home, whom she hated. There was something wrong about him and she could remember hiding from him whenever he visited her parents. But, strangely, even though she was so obviously frightened of this man, her mother continued to ask him to baby-sit. When, much later, Mrs P had asked her mother why she had continued to use that baby-sitter, of whom she was so clearly frightened, she was told that it didn't seem to matter as long as she was asleep when he came. (I gathered that her parents sometimes went down to the pub in the late evening, at which times this neighbour used to baby-sit for them.) But Mrs P then remembered, with great alarm, that she had woken up to find herself alone with this man in her bedroom. She was quite small. She was also sure that this had happened on several occasions.

So, the man in my waiting-room had come to represent the man next door, this neighbour. And I, as the person who had not stopped him intruding upon the patient, had become the mother who was allowing something intolerable to continue happening. A few months later in the analysis it became clear that there had been actual sexual interference by this neighbour. Thus, through a chance real event in relation to the analysis, this patient had begun to get in touch with that traumatic experience, and eventually to remember.

The feelings about that repeated trauma could now be worked through in the transference. However, I had first to regain my position as an analyst who could be more alert and sensitive to what was happening to the patient. Only then could she feel safe enough to use me, and the events that had impinged upon her analysis, to represent those other realities of her inner world, and for the memories of her childhood trauma to be recovered from repression.

Conclusion

In the examples I have given there is always more than one reality operating. There is the reality of 'environmental provision', in the analysis as well as childhood, and there is the reality of the inner world. But that inner reality is also partly based upon early environmental realities – in terms of which much subsequent experience may be perceived and interpreted. Thus, Mr L (*example 8.1*) saw all relationships, particularly any that might be caring, as a potential threat; and Miss M (*example 8.2*) had come to regard anyone she experienced as a mother as someone who would be cruel to her.

There is also a distortion of how external reality is perceived, due to what is projected on to others, and I have indicated how this had to be allowed for in thinking about any account of childhood experiences – as with Miss M. And yet, not all bad experience with others can be attributed to such projections. How the analyst works can also become a bad experience, especially if the effects of this are not acknowledged or remedied by the analyst, which can lead to impasse or breakdown in the analysis.

In addition, there is the overlapping of different realities that will inevitably occur as part of the analytic process. Here there are triggers for transference, with transference elaborations by the patient that result in aspects of his/her past being relived within the analytic relationship. But not all that is experienced in relation to the analyst is transference.

Unconscious re-enactment by the analyst, if it is attended to, can sometimes have an important diagnostic function, as when the analyst's failure represents a key feature in the patient's past. It may thus represent what is needing to be dealt with in the analysis – and dealt with in a new way, which can help to relegate the past to the past, as with Mrs P (*example 8.3*).

I have, in particular, wished to emphasize *the analyst's own part in the analytic process*, and the need for recognizing the

Chapter nine

Trial identification and technique[1]

Once we accept the fact that the analytic process is affected by the impact of the analyst's way of working, it becomes important that the analyst can develop ways of monitoring the possible effects of this, from the patient's point of view. Examples are given, and technical 'exercises' suggested for interest's sake, which can help to heighten an awareness of this dimension to the analytic relationship.

Introduction

A central issue in analysis is the freedom to work with the transference, to be able to interpret to the patient those ways in which the past is spilling into the present – affecting the patient's perceptions of the other and therefore his/her ways of relating. But for this interpretive work to be convincing to a patient, it is important that the objective realities in the analytic relationship do not mask or blur these manifestations of transference. It is therefore useful for analysts and therapists to monitor the ways in which they work with their patients so that they can recognize more readily the extent to which patients' responses are determined as much by these objective realities as by what is transferred to the analyst.

In the course of running clinical workshops, and in supervision, I have sometimes used clinical vignettes to create opportunities for practising technique. When musicians are having difficulty in playing a particular passage, they often break the problem down into manageable 'bits' in order to see where the difficulty lies. And, having identified this, they invent 'technical exercises' in order to develop fluency in playing difficult passages. This use of exercises – for practice outside the consulting-room – is likewise useful in clinical practice. For it is when the analyst is *with* a patient, and under the pressures that are often an integral part of experiencing the patient's presence, that it is least possible to have this freedom to reflect and to explore the technical implications of how we might respond to the patient.

I have been referring to trial identification from time to time throughout this book, and I have already described in some detail the different uses of trial identification (see Chapter 4). I now wish to focus more extensively upon *trial identification with the patient in the session* in order to get a better sense of how the patient may be experiencing the analyst, in what is being said or in the analyst's manner in the session, and how the patient may hear (or mishear) what the analyst has it in mind to say.

Some examples

I shall first mention some common technical issues illustrating the value, in relation to technique, of trial identification with the patient in the session.

The timing of transference interpretations

One of the most frequent problems of technique is that of the timing of transference interpretations. If we consider the implications of such interpretations from the patient's point of view, it becomes easier to distinguish between those occasions when the patient needs a transference interpretation without delay and other times when it is important not to interpret too quickly.

For instance, if a patient is caught up in a transference to the analyst as someone felt to be hostile to the point where this is threatening the analytic work, then of course it is important to identify where this transference comes from (having first checked that it is not based upon some objective reality in how the analyst has been speaking to the patient). That interpreting of the transference can free the patient to continue with the analysis, which might otherwise have become blocked. Similarly, if a patient is beginning to get caught up in an erotized transference, it is important not to delay in interpreting this for what it signifies.

However, there are times when a patient gets into strong feelings (such as anger or hating) which key figures in the patient's past may not have been able to tolerate. At such times it could be a mistake to interpret straight away that these feelings really belong to someone other than the analyst. Instead, it can become a valuable experience if the analyst stays with these feelings long enough to demonstrate that they can be taken on the chin, as if they did belong solely to the analyst (see *example 8.3*). Otherwise, he/she may be experienced by the patient as being too much like others before, also unable to bear being the object of such feelings. By waiting long enough before interpreting the transference here, a number of gains may follow: first, the details of the transference experience now being relived may become clearer, so that a more specific interpretation later becomes possible; also, the patient is able to have the experience of being with someone who is not backing off from a difficult experience. That can help to alter the quality of the patient's feelings here: they can be recognized as a form of communication; they do not have to be sheltered from or retaliated against. So it is often important to recognize when a transference interpretation (if given too immediately) could be perceived by the patient as the analyst being defensive, as if he/she were saying: 'Don't give *that* to me – it doesn't belong to *me*.'

A typical example of staying with a patient's anger (say) may be found in dealing with a patient's reactions to a cancelled session. The absence has been real; it may also have come at a particularly bad time for the patient. The reasons for the patient finding this so difficult may reflect feelings about a sudden absence in childhood. Nevertheless, staying with the anger – as if it were only to do with the analyst's absence – often results in the emergence of fresh details about earlier desertions or absences. I think that opportunities are lost when a patient's anger is too quickly interpreted 'away' from the analyst, as if it were all to do with some specific earlier experience. That is usually already known about. But more important details (perhaps of other absences) may still need to be discovered, and these often surface when the analyst accepts the immediate focus for the patient's feeling, such as the untimeliness of a cancelled session for that particular patient, as if it might not have been transference at all. Subsequent experience often demonstrates the value of having allowed that fuller transference experience to develop, particularly when the patient needs to find that this is after all manageable by the analyst. However, at other times a patient will need early interpretation in order to feel contained. The problem is to discern which timing is likely to be most fruitful under which circumstances.

The therapist is experienced as critical

Example 9.1

Suppose a patient has told us what he is thinking, and we feel that there is something strange about this which needs to be explored further. If we were then to say 'Why do you think that?', how might a patient hear this apparently quite simple question?

First of all, because it is a question, there is an implied pressure upon the patient to reply. But, in this context, the question could also be felt as criticism. The patient could hear the question as indicating that he should *not* be thinking in the way he has just described. He might then feel a need to justify this by defensively offering an explanation.

So, rather than ask a question here, we could simply make a statement (not requiring an answer) such as: 'I wonder why you think this.' But truly, although it is partly disguised it is still a question, even if in a gentler form.

We might just say: 'You have some reason for thinking this'; or, 'I am not yet clear about this.' The patient can then help us to become clearer (or not) as he wishes.

The therapist is experienced as defensive

Example 9.2

A patient has been describing a number of recent experiences in which she felt criticized. The therapist (a man) recognized that these could be displaced references to the transference. But he puts this as a question: 'Do you expect me to criticize you too?' The patient immediately replied: 'Oh, no: I know that you wouldn't be critical.'

If we look at the therapist's response from the patient's point of view, we can readily sense that the question here is *expecting* the answer 'No'. The patient might then see the therapist as unwilling to accept that she could, in fact, be expecting him to be critical. A statement here would more clearly allow the patient a freedom to enter into the transference without being quite so anxious about whether the therapist could tolerate this. For example, the therapist could have said: 'You are telling me about your experiences of being criticized. I think you may be expecting me to be critical too.' The patient could then feel able to say that she does expect this, and she might go on to give examples from recent sessions when she had already been experiencing the therapist as critical. And that, in turn, might prompt the therapist to reflect upon the possible basis for that sense of being criticized.

With the benefit of a patient's feed-back, we may also find that some implicit criticism had been conveyed in the manner of recent interpretations. And, if that had been the case, it is then important that the therapist find some way of dealing with that reality without treating all of the patient's experience as transference. That does not mean, necessarily, that the therapist should always admit to what his/her feelings may have been. It is often sufficient, in such a situation, to say: 'I can see how you could have heard what I said as critical.' Acknowledging the reality is sometimes a better way of approaching the transference. To focus first, and only, on the transference will be seen by the patient as defensive – even as the therapist denying the elements of objective reality in the analytic relationship. It is always detrimental to the working alliance to give that impression to a patient.

The therapist is experienced as intrusive

Example 9.3

Patient (a woman): 'I had a dream about some kind of sexual encounter. It was quite confusing. There were two sexual organs in some kind of contact. They seemed disembodied as if they did not belong to anybody. I think that one organ must have been mine but I do not know whose the other was. The situation seemed dangerous. I think that there was a risk of some infection, but I do not know whether it was the man who was infected or me.'

Therapist (a man): 'Was there anything else in the dream?'

We can use this brief interchange for practice. If we trial-identify with the patient and consider the implication of this response by the therapist – what is the impression that we get? First, the question is intrusive. It also suggests that the therapist wants more. Further, if we consider the quality of the question in this particular context we can see that it could be experienced by the patient as voyeuristic. How then are we to assess the patient's response?

To the question 'Was there anything else in the dream?' the patient replied: 'Not really. I don't think that there was any actual intercourse. But I think it may have taken place by an open window – somewhere you could look into.'

We might therefore wonder whether it was just coincidence that the patient replied in this way: it sounds almost as if she is apologizing to the therapist for disappointing his voyeuristic expectations. But she adds that the sexual encounter took place 'somewhere you could look into'. This too speaks to the therapist as if he were unconsciously perceived as having a salacious interest in peering into the patient's sexual activities. I regard this as a clear illustration of 'unconscious supervision by the patient'.

Different uses of the countertransference

Example 9.4

A therapist working in a therapeutic community found himself feeling very impatient with a particular resident. This resident had been frequently absent from community meetings, sometimes absent for a day or several days at a time, so that it was not clear whether she had really left, or what was happening.

The therapist eventually confronted this girl very directly with her behaviour: 'I cannot put up with any more of this coming and going, and the effects that this is having on the community, as it leaves us not knowing what has happened to you.'

The intention of the confrontation was to set a limit to this disturbing and quite destructive behaviour. It may even have been the most effective way of dealing with that particular resident at the time. We can nevertheless use this example for some practice. For instance, if we listen to the form of the therapist's statement we can readily recognize the superego quality of it: the resident should not go on behaving in this way.

Now, under some circumstances, this kind of confrontation could be quite appropriate if a patient needs to be faced with the implications of difficult behaviour, even if this means that the therapist intermittently becomes an auxiliary superego to the patient. This could arise if the patient's own superego control is either absent or so severe that it is defensively disowned (projected), which can have the effect of inducing in others a superego response that appears then to have come from 'outside' the patient rather than from 'inside'.

When I learned that this particular resident had been abandoned by her natural parents, had been fostered but then placed in a series of children's homes, it was possible to see the countertransference response here in a different light. The therapist had been affected by the resident's repeated 'comings' and 'goings', and he was beginning to feel angry about these – confused and not knowing what was happening. It is possible then to see that the resident may unconsciously have been communicating something of her own distress and confusion about the comings and goings in *her* life. Perhaps, by means of her absences, she had been stirring up feelings in others that echoed her own unmanageable feelings about absences, which others (through projective identification) were picking up in her stead.

With this in mind it is possible to consider other ways in which the therapist might have responded. He might have been able to draw upon his own feelings in order to offer to the resident the thought that she might have been behaving towards the community as others had towards her. It would be possible then to consider how she probably had similar difficult feelings in response to other absences and other losses in her life. Her behaviour could thus have been recognized as a form of communication rather than being treated as difficult behaviour. And if she *had* been communicating unmanageable feelings, then we can see that the therapist's reaction to this could have been experienced by her as evidence that he too was unable to bear them.

Interpreting behaviour as communication

One of the problems about interpreting behaviour as communication is that a patient is often so sensitive to anything like criticism that almost any interpretation is likely to be experienced first as criticism. Of course it is possible to interpret that reaction by a patient as evidence of transference, which it almost certainly is, but when that happens too often it can deflect from what might have been a more fruitful exploration of the communication that the behaviour had conveyed. There clearly are times when the more important communication is to be found in the behaviour rather than in a possible transference from critical parents.

How much to put into an interpretation

Not all interpretations need to be as long or as full as they sometimes are. When they are too full we can usefully wonder about the implications of this for the patient.

Example 9.5

A trainee therapist in analysis with me had been upset that his first training patient had already left therapy whereas he still needed to be in analysis. I knew that my patient had been quite seriously deprived by his own inattentive mother who had consistently disregarded his need for her attention. I therefore interpreted: 'I think it is possible that you get something out of your patients still needing you, maybe because it gives you a way of being the attentive mother to your patient seen as a needy child – doing for someone else what your mother seems not to have done for you.'

Now, if we look at my interpretation we can see that I have done more of the analytic work for the patient than is really necessary. I could have left the interpretation with just the first part: 'I think it is possible that you get something out of your patients still needing you. . . .' Leaving it there could have left the patient to do his own analytic work around this observation. As it was, the patient's response to this mostly echoed what I had said, which prompted me to realize that I had said too much.

A balance between not-knowing and being firm

When might it be most useful to make interpretations that leave the patient free to explore further and when is it more appropriate to make an interpretation that is more definite?

There are certainly times when it is better to make a statement that can be challenged, in particular in the area of character defences (those things about the self that the patient least wants to acknowledge), because the resistance to facing painful truth about the self is unlikely to shift if the form of an interpretation is too mild, too tentative. Also, it is important for the analyst to offer understanding with a sufficient sureness to be able to contain a patient in crisis.

However, if the analyst's whole style of working appears to be based upon certainty, this will have far-reaching implications. A patient has then to do battle with the analyst's dogmatic attitude, with the risk of being beaten down by the analyst who can always have the last word – 'the analyst (like some parents) always knows best', or the patient may give up and comply. A greater possibility for creative interchange is at times preserved when the patient is invited to respond to the analyst's shared not-knowing or to play with half-interpretations. Then the patient, as someone invited to take part in the working alliance, can work with the analyst towards fuller (and shared) understanding.

I shall not be giving examples of this here but analysts and therapists can readily find their own.

Interpretations that re-enact

Not infrequently the analyst or therapist gets drawn into a re-enactment with the patient to a point where even the attempts at interpreting become a part of that re-enactment. It is useful to scan for the potential re-enactment that may be concealed within the form of interpretation that may first come to mind.

One of the more common ways in which interpretations can become a re-enactment is in the realm of sexual abuse. It is well known that rape victims (and it must also be true of child-abuse victims) experience the subsequent police questioning as a repetition of the original trauma. Analysts have to be watchful that they do not do something similar when they interpret sexual matters to such a patient (see *example 2.6*).

When there has been incest in a patient's childhood there is a strong unconscious push to repeat aspects of that trauma in the transference, as a way of communicating this to the analyst. Sometimes the trauma has been 'forgotten' and only re-emerges into consciousness through these partial repetitions, but there are many pitfalls on the way to recovering such memories.

Not infrequently an incest-victim has experienced a double trauma, not only suffering an abusing father but also a mother who remained blind to the abuse of her own child (see *example 8.3*). The analyst is then faced with many problems of tact and timing. If the analyst interprets too swiftly, and too confidently, that the patient's free associations suggest something sexual – let alone assuming anything so specific as sexual interference by a parent – this attempt at interpreting may be experienced as forcing a sexual meaning upon the patient's more innocent-seeming associations.[2]

There is the counterpart problem – that of delaying too long before verbalizing the sexual implications of a patient's communications, and how these seem to point to something incestuous. Too long a delay in acknowledging what can no longer be overlooked can be experienced by the patient as the analyst being afraid to face facts: the analyst may then seem to have become a re-enactment of the mother who turned a blind eye to what had been happening.

Some technical exercises

The following 'exercises' are offered for practice. They are not given as models for technique, but in the hope that they may inspire readers to make up their own exercises to heighten their awareness of the patient's point of view.

Identification with the aggressor

A particular form of communication through behaviour is evident when patients communicate something of their own experience through an identification with the aggressor. A patient may then behave towards the analyst in ways that represent some hurtful treatment the patient had previously experienced. By practising with the different ways of trying to interpret this behaviour we might find a way that does not too readily evoke the more likely response of feeling criticized.

> Exercise A
>
> A male patient has been putting the analyst down, attacking every interpretation to the point where the analyst is beginning to feel that whatever she says will be wrong. What are the options?

The analyst might feel like saying: 'Whatever I say today seems to be wrong' and this could be justified in terms of confronting the patient. The intention here could be for the analyst to identify the transference, trying to understand this in terms of how someone has treated the patient in this kind of way. But if we put ourselves in the shoes of the patient, we can sense the quality of this response as critical, as complaining, and perhaps as retaliatory. How might a patient respond to that?

If the patient were then to say that he/she feels criticized, or attacked, by the analyst's confrontation we could not necessarily assume that this also points to some transference (see also *example 9.2*). It could of course be that some unconscious role-responsiveness was evoked in the analyst whereby she had become an embodiment of a complaining parent, and there is the possibility of some fruitful analysis along those lines. This would lead naturally to an interpretation of the patient's use of 'identification with the aggressor' which may also be conveyed in this behaviour and which it might be more important to understand.

It might however be more fruitful if we could find a way of approaching the patient's behaviour that does not so predictably make the patient feel criticized. If that response is predictable I think we should wonder how much of it would necessarily be transference: some of it may be set up by the analyst's mode of intervention.

Another way of approaching this kind of problem is found through *creating an atmosphere of understanding* (as in *example 8.2*) before attempting to confront the patient. The analyst could, for instance, start by saying something like: 'I think that you may be communicating something to me in the only way that you can – by behaving towards me as your father (or mother) may have behaved towards you.' The wish to understand the unconscious communication in this behaviour is then clearly demonstrated as the priority, rather than any wish to criticize the patient for it, and the patient is likely to have a fuller sense of this and to respond accordingly.

Or the analyst could offer an interpretation first and then point to the basis for it in the patient's behaviour. He could say: 'I get the impression that you have had the experience of being often put in the wrong, and I think that that is why you have been putting me in a similar position in this session.'

If, however, we practise further we might notice that this last interpretation (like so many) contains two statements rather than one. A further option could be to leave the patient with the first half only, to see what the patient does with it. One patient might take that up immediately with detail from the childhood, which could later be linked with the re-enactment of this in the analytic relationship; another patient might first want to question where the analyst gets that impression from and, having been told, might then give detail from the childhood. Also, we might note, the fuller interpretation runs the risk of pre-empting a focus by the patient upon the analytic relationship (a common analytic preference) rather than leaving it open for the patient to respond to the first part of the interpretation in whichever way first occurs to the patient.

There is, of course, no particular 'right way'. In all these so-called exercises there is always a possibility of choice in how to interpret.

The order of an interpretation

An interesting point of technique which the exercise above can also illustrate is *the effect of order in an interpretation*. By choosing an order that is careful not to create a diversion (for instance through the patient's response to a sense of being criticized) it may be possible to explore something new in the analysis. If the patient still responds with feeling criticized then it would be clearer that this really is transference. Trial identification with the patient, before interpreting, can often help to highlight where a patient's sensitivities might lie and can help to point to different ways of interpreting and the possible implications of each (as in Chapter 4).

Re-establishing the analytic space

For analytic work to be possible there has to be sufficient analytic space within which the patient and analyst can together reflect upon what is happening in the session. There are times, however, when this gets lost and needs to be re-established.

Exercise B

In supervision I encountered a stalemate in a session in which the female therapist and a female patient each felt that she was being double-bound by the other, and there seemed to be no way out of that without both parties getting into some kind of 'You started it' interaction. How might one try to get out of that stalemate?

I thought it worth doing some practice with this vignette during that supervision. The analytic space had been temporarily lost, so we might think of some way in which this could be re-established. Or, maybe, we could find a way of offering the patient some transitional space in which analytic reflection could be resumed. One might share an idea with the patient that could be played with, such as: 'I am getting an image here of a parent and a child who are locked in a stalemate – with each blaming the other for what is happening between them.' The patient might recognize enough validity in that to respond from her own experience. This might then lead to some clarification of which childhood experience(s) had been spilling into the present, trapping both parties in much the same way as had happened in the past. Enough analytic space might then be restored to explore the interaction between therapist and patient without continuing to prolong it through a process of mutual blame.

Internal supervision may make it possible to find a reflective viewpoint from which to explore the interaction rather than to remain caught up in it.

Linking the past and the present

Psychoanalytic interpretation is always at some level making links between the past and the present. It is, however, not always remembered that the *direction of an interpretation* has different implications for the patient. And again we are most likely to recognize the difference if we monitor from the patient's point of view what we might be about to say or what has just been said.

Exercise C

A patient comes to a session very angry, shouting at me for my absence of two weeks over the Easter holiday: 'You were not here when I most needed you.' I recognize the link with her past experience of abandonment, her mother having gone on holiday with her new baby leaving the older child (my patient) in the care of relatives. There are many ways in which I could make links here, so let us look at the contrasting implications for the patient in how the past and the present here might be interpreted as connected.

I could interpret: 'You are angry with me now because I have been away and this has reminded you of the time when your mother left you shortly after your brother was born.' The 'direction' of this interpretation takes the focus away from myself (in the present) back into the patient's past. The patient might therefore feel that I could be deflecting her angry shouting away from me on to her mother, as if I were saying: 'You are not really angry with me but with your mother.' The patient could then see me as afraid of her feelings. She might then either become even more uncontained with her anger (if no one else can manage this then how can she?); or she might suppress her anger, or keep it deflected away from me, for fear that I might not be able to cope with such direct expressions of strong feelings. Clearly this is not the conscious intention of making an interpretation that has a direction towards the past. But it does often happen that interpretations are given in this mode, and I think the implications of that direction towards the past are not noticed often enough or monitored.

Another way of making the same interpretive link is to start with the past detail and to follow the direction of the transference – where the past is spilling into the present. We can then help the patient to see what it is that is happening in the session whilst at the same time being more clearly prepared to stay with those difficult feelings *in the present* until they come to be experienced by the patient as more contained. We could say: 'At a time when you were most dependent upon your mother she went away with your brother. You were feeling particularly dependent upon me before the Easter break and then I went away, so you experience me now as the mother who left you when you most needed her.' This way round offers some insight into the present distress whilst keeping the immediate focus still in the present where the patient's feelings are being expressed.

What I have said here, about linking past and present, applies equally to the use of material from a previous session. If there is something difficult in the present session, and the analyst makes a link between this and an earlier session, this linking can sometimes be seen by the patient as a defensive manoeuvre by the analyst – moving to the safer ground of clinical archaeology (the dead history of a past session) rather than staying with what is happening in the present. If it still seems useful, or necessary, to bring in something from an earlier session I think it is important to try to find a way of introducing it so that the focus remains quite clearly in the present. And if the patient's attention shifts from the present to the earlier session referred to, or in some other way remains focused outside the current interaction with the analyst, then it may be that the patient is giving the analyst an unconscious cue to recognize the deflective effects of a reference at that moment to something more safely in the past. It is always helpful if the analyst can recognize when the patient is reacting in this kind of way and to be alert to the possible reasons why.

It is well worth remembering that we do not need to go in search of the past: the unconscious brings the past to us – through the past becoming dynamically present in the session. The interpretive task is then to understand which elements of the patient's past are being re-experienced now, and why.

The use of strong terms

Not infrequently we have patients use strong terms in describing themselves or others. I think that it is worth thinking about some of the problems that can develop around using a patient's language – when to use it too and when not to.

Exercise D

A patient has been describing her new boss who, she insists, is obstructive to her work. The therapist refers to this description in his interpretation: 'I see that you are having difficulties with this obstructive boss.' What are the implications in this for the patient?

The patient could feel that the therapist accepts her own perception of the boss as obstructive – without question. This could temporarily limit the analytic space in which to analyse the patient's perception, and we do need to be able to wonder how valid that perception is. Whose obstructiveness is being referred to in the session? The boss's? The patient's in projection? And/or some transference on to the boss seen as obstructive? Or might this be a displacement from the therapist who may recently have been experienced in this way?

One way of keeping open the analytic space here would be for the therapist to play back the patient's description more clearly as the patient's perception: 'You put great emphasis on how obstructive he seems to be.' Or the therapist could make some comment such as: 'A key theme in what you are saying is around someone being obstructive', thus opening up the question of whose obstructiveness is being alluded to. This does not presume that the focus is to be on the external world or upon the internal world of the patient. There is then plenty of room for the patient to take this observation further and for various other possible dimensions to be included in the analytic investigation.

We might also note, in passing, that for the therapist to accept too quickly that it is the boss who is being seen as obstructive could be an unconscious way of deflecting this criticism away from the therapist.

Exercise E

A patient has been talking to his therapist about himself and makes a reference to what he calls 'my shitty feelings'. The therapist adopts the patient's language here and makes an interpretation in which he speaks of 'your shitty feelings' to the patient. How might the patient hear this?

It is possible that the patient could feel some relief that the therapist is accepting his own view of himself. Where else can that lead? Of course, without other detail we cannot know. But we can also sense that the patient might regard this use of his own self-description as confirming that his feelings really are 'shitty'. The therapist may have been invited into a judgemental attitude towards the patient which could be a re-enactment from the past. But what about the analytic space? Has the patient the necessary freedom to examine this view of his feelings? If the therapist seems to see his feelings in the same way as the patient does, then what more is there to say about them? 'They are shitty', so that would be that!

By contrast, we might consider how to address the patient's self-view without speaking as if it were being accepted as the only possible view. For instance the therapist could say: 'You have come to regard your feelings as shitty . . .', which could lead to an exploration into how this has come about. Or, the therapist could say: 'I think you expect me also to see your feelings as shitty . . .', which could lead to wondering about this invitation to have the therapist become the critical parent, or whoever. In either case there is more analytic space created here by the therapist addressing the same thing as the patient (the 'shitty' feelings) without seeming to adopt the same perspective. The analytic work can evolve within that analytic space in a way that is less likely to happen if these feelings were just spoken of as shitty, as if that were the only way to speak of them, or as if there were no work to be done on how these feelings have come to be regarded in this way.

It is important, however, to be able to recognize when strong terms do need to be used, even if these are introduced by the analyst, and it is useful to notice examples when that is necessary. But how these strong terms are introduced will make a difference to how the patient is likely to experience them.

Exercise F

A patient has been complaining about other people putting him down and he has been feeling rather persecuted by this. He has also not been able to see why people have been treating him in this way.

His therapist has been aware of an arrogance in his patient and tries to point out that other people may be reacting to this. He says: 'I think that people may have been reacting to your arrogance by putting you in your place.'

There are a number of things we can notice about this, if we use it as an exercise, again bearing in mind that we do not have any background detail. For instance, we do not know if this is an old theme (that of arrogance), in which case this comment may be an entirely appropriate confrontation. Or, if the patient is someone who takes little notice of comments that are made with less impact than this, there may be a case for using a statement more likely to get through to him and for the therapist to deal with the consequences. On the other hand, if this is the first time that arrogance has been mentioned in the therapy it could feel to the patient as a further put-down, this time by the therapist.

With some patients the more important focus for analysis needs to be less upon the fact of arrogance than upon the reasons for this – in other words on the defensive function of arrogance. A less combative atmosphere is preserved, for shared work on such a defence, if some way can be found which also communicates an awareness of the insecurity that lies behind the arrogance. One way could be to say something like: 'I think that a problem here is that when you are feeling threatened you try to appear big. Other people then see you as being arrogant without realizing that you are protecting yourself from feeling small.' This is by no means the only way to tackle such an issue, but I give this alternative interpretation to illustrate the different quality in this compared to the potentially more hurtful confrontation used in the example.

Beware assumptions

It is all too easy for analysts and therapists to fall into making assumptions which can deprive the patient of an important freedom to put things in his/her own way. Often these assumptions are left unchallenged by the patient.

Exercise G

I notice sometimes in supervision that a therapist evaluates an experience for the patient. For instance a therapist may say: 'You must have found that very upsetting.' What if the patient had not found it 'very upsetting'?

I think that it is often better for the patient to be the one to add the word 'very' rather than have to deal with the therapist's assumption that the patient's reaction will have been extreme. Of course, such a comment will not matter when the patient's experience was as assumed, but we may not discover when it is different if the form of an interpretation has been evaluative on behalf of the patient.

By contrast it leaves a patient more room to make his/her own evaluation of an experience if the therapist approaches this without assumptions. The therapist could ask: 'How did you feel about that?' But that is a question and the patient is likely to feel it must be answered. Or, the therapist might make a statement such as: 'I am not clear what you felt about this.' As this is no more than an observation, and about the present limit of the therapist's understanding, the patient can feel invited to clarify what was felt, if anything.

However, if a patient has been in a situation that was almost certainly distressing, I think that it is necessary to find some way of acknowledging that feelings may have run high without assuming what kind of feelings these were. 'You probably felt pretty strongly about this' can leave room for the patient to fill in with the detail of these feelings, which could range from feeling angry, frightened, guilty, excited – or whatever. If the therapist assumes that the patient would have felt anger, when it had been excitement that was felt, the patient is sometimes going to be inhibited from admitting to that. Also, if a therapist says: 'You must have felt very guilty about this', it is likely that a patient will hear this as saying that this is what *should* have been felt. It does not always follow that this is how it was.

A patient whose younger sibling had died soon after birth could be assumed to have problems about guilt. But, in the early stages of getting to know such a patient, it is important not to assume that the patient is aware of this. 'I wonder how you felt about this death' allows the patient to reflect upon it and perhaps to come out with a very different (and important) revelation, such as: 'Well, actually, I remember feeling a great sense of relief. . . . I would not have to put up with a rival after all.' If the therapist had assumed that the primary feelings would have been those of guilt it is unlikely that the patient will easily confess to these other feelings. There may then be induced guilt, or guilt at not having felt guilt, which is quite another matter.

Interpreting unconscious guilt

Exercise H

A patient had been raging against her hated husband. She could see no good in him at all. She would really like to get rid of him but she could not make him leave nor could she find anywhere to go if she left him. Then the husband had a heart attack and died. Following this, the patient clearly switched into a reaction formation against her former hatred, arranging an elaborate funeral and speaking nothing but praise for her dead husband. But she soon developed a crippling skin rash which she felt was threatening to drive her crazy. The therapist eventually made a link between the rash and her unconscious guilt. He said: 'I think that you are unconsciously punishing yourself with this rash because you feel so bad about the hate that you used to feel for your husband before he died. Now, instead of attacking him, you are attacking yourself with the rash which is causing you so much distress.' How might the patient experience this interpretation?

In the shoes of the patient we might expect her to feel criticized by this, even attacked by it, and that is almost certainly why she stopped coming to see her therapist. From that day she refused to see him again. (As a colleague once said of this kind of interpretation: 'That is just adding insight to injury.')

We therefore need to anticipate a patient's likely reaction under similar circumstances so that we can interpret from a more neutral position. And we must remember that a patient's superego attacks at such times are often already so acute that it takes very little for an interpretation to be heard as from the superego in projection. To help deal with this it is necessary to be especially careful not to interpret in a way that is likely to amplify that process and to blur the distinction between external and internal realities.

When trying to interpret unconscious guilt I have found it helpful to use what I 'know' analytically to find a way of approaching this through not (yet) knowing. For instance, if I were to have said to this patient: 'You seem to be suffering a great deal from this rash' the patient might well have agreed, and she might have added other details of suffering. Eventually I might have been able to point out a more specific quality in these different forms of suffering: 'It is almost as if you are experiencing this suffering as some kind of punishment.' And, at some stage, I might even share the thought: 'But, it is not clear what you are feeling guilty about.' The patient might then feel free to explore this sense of guilt about something, perhaps still non-specific, or may begin talking about her mixed feelings for her husband about whom she used to be so nasty. At least the patient would not be so likely to feel that she was with someone who expected her to feel guilty, as if siding with the patient's superego, as the patient in the example probably felt.

The therapist could have taken more care not to side with the connection that the patient is making, between her having expressed some wish for the husband's death and his dying. When guilt is a reaction to this kind of false connection, based upon magical thinking, then we have to be careful that we do not appear to be assuming the same connection. If we speak as if we see the guilt and the connection all too clearly, from the patient's point of view that can be experienced as if we too believe that this is how the husband's death had been brought about, by her expressions of hate for him. Contrarily, 'not knowing' the connection, but finding it in the patient's own communications, can help towards analysing the unconscious guilt from a position that is not accepting any link between death and death-wishing as causal.

Other clinical situations

There are countless clinical events that we encounter in our daily work which can be used for practising technique, creating 'exercises' such as I have illustrated above, exploring each from the point of view of the patient. For instance:

– interpreting acting out (experienced as an attempt to contain through understanding or through superego control?)

– dealing with different kinds of silence (the risk of being intrusive or of being seen as retaliating with silence – the need to recognize the differences between silence as 'being with', silence as resistance or as communication, etc.)

– dealing with a dilemma (recognizing that attention given to *this* could be seen by the patient as neglecting *that*, and vice versa)

– exploring the dynamics of reassurance (the patient's difficult feelings being seen as too much for the therapist)

– commenting on a patient's lateness (seen as attending to the communication in this or as rebuking the patient?)

– dealing with the therapist's lateness – offering make-up time (being fair or buying off the patient's anger?)

– offering an extra session at a time of acute distress (meeting a patient's need or communicating the therapist's view of the patient as not able to cope?)

– suggesting medication (seen as a necessary containment or as protecting the therapist from the patient's distress?)

– dealing with direct questions from the patient (seen as defensive in not answering or as seductive in doing so?).

The list could be endless.

Conclusion

Technical exercises such as those presented here may help us to see similar situations more readily when in the consulting-room. We may also be able to see more clearly why with a particular patient we might handle a difficult situation in one way and with another perhaps quite differently. This use of trial identification can therefore help us to work more specifically with the individual patient rather than fall into well-worn ways of thinking and interpreting. Herein lies the fascination in developing psychoanalytic technique and the reason why trying to find therapeutic ways of working within the analytic encounter remains for ever challenging.

Chapter ten

The analytic space and process

Some underlying themes of this book are highlighted here – two in particular: the nature of the mental and emotional space, which is provided by the analytic relationship, and the dynamics of the analytic process itself. It is suggested that, when the analytic space is kept sufficiently free from influences that could distort and disable it, the process that then unfolds can be trusted and followed.

> The frame marks off the different kind of reality that is within it from that which is outside it; but a temporal spatial frame also marks off the special kind of reality of a psycho-analytic session. And in psycho-analysis it is the existence of this frame that makes possible the full development of that creative illusion that analysts call transference.
>
> (Milner 1952: 183)

Introduction

The mental and emotional space between people tends to be eroded by the claims that each person makes upon the other. The analytic space is unique in protecting the patient from such claims. The space within the analytic frame is kept separate from the world outside, allowing that particular kind of relating to develop in which the transference can freely emerge. Through the transference, the past experience of the patient represented in his/her internal world comes to be relived in the analytic relationship. It is this which so vividly brings into focus the ways whereby the patient's past still continues to spill into the present. In order to see these manifestations of transference most clearly, the world within this frame is protected as far as possible from influences other than those that emanate from the patient's past.

158

If sufficient care is not given to this protection, the analyst can become a prime source of interfering influence. The analytic space will then be impaired and the analytic process deflected and/or distorted.

The analytic process is not created by the analyst. It has a dynamic of its own, a direction that expresses unconscious hope or the unconscious search of the patient, and often it seems to contain unconscious wisdom.

Analytic space

Rules and the analytic space

The analytic space needs to be protected from both external and internal influence. This protection is primarily provided by the arrangements for the analytic work.

The consulting-room space gives privacy and protection from intrusion by others; the set times, kept specifically for each patient, provide reliability and continuity; the professional ethic offers a guaranteed confidentiality and non-exploitation of the patient; and the relative anonymity of the analyst aims to keep to a minimum the impact upon the patient of knowing personal details about him/her. Normally, this framework can be taken for granted but many patients have to test it for themselves.

However, the analytic space is much more than this: it acknowledges the need for boundaries between people, and therefore respects a patient's need for boundaries, including those that are still needed to protect the ego from whatever it is not yet able to manage. When the need for such defences has been sufficiently analysed and understood, and when the patient is ready, they will be relinquished. They do not need to be removed by the analyst. The analytic space also offers a freedom from the intrusive pressures (influence, reassurance, advice, or moral judgement) that could arise from any personal or theoretical predisposition of the analyst. Pressure of any kind, in particular any sense of 'ought' or 'should' from the analyst, is antithetical to analysis, and so are preconceptions when these overrule the patient's experience and perception.

There are no rules for the patient. The only variation from this, which rarely has to be made explicit, is that communication can be in any form except through violence or physical contact. The only rules (in analysis) are those for the analyst, in particular those that protect the patient's space.

Freud never quite freed himself from some use of pressure: he still advocated the 'fundamental rule' of free association. But his emphasis upon any departure from this (as a manifestation of resistance) could have the effect of bullying the patient, as if to say: 'If you do not associate freely – we have ways of making you.'[1] The concept and value of analytic space has therefore only gradually become apparent since Freud, and it was many years before Margaret Little said: 'We no longer "require" our patients to tell us everything that is in their minds. On the contrary, we give them permission to do so' (Little 1951: 39).

The need for space

The need, in analysis, for mental and emotional space is highlighted by the comparative absence of space in other relationships. To be healthy, every intimate relationship needs space and personal boundaries, and a corresponding respect by each person for the 'otherness' of the other. Frequently, however, this space is either lacking or contaminated by intruding influences.

All parents, however well-intentioned, will impose pressures upon a child that come from needs and wishes of their own. With an infant, there will be such pressures as a wish for the baby to feed when expected, a wish for the baby to settle when convenient, and a need for the mother to be confirmed as a good mother by appreciative responses from her baby. The list could be endless. As we all know, such wishes and needs are not always met by the infant, nor should they be! But if a mother's expectations are too insistent, they can eventually result in compliant behaviour and an impaired autonomy.[2]

With the older child, the wishes and needs of parents can be just as pressing but they are often more complex: a wish to see the child develop in a given way, a wish to influence choices, a need to be loved by the child: and so on. In all subsequent relationships, whether between friends, teacher and pupil, employer and employee, lovers or marital partners, etc., there will always be a pressure from each for some fitting into expectations, regardless of the needs of the other.

In these relationships there is less of the space that is typical of the analytic relationship. There may be physical space, leaving the other person alone, but that does not necessarily meet the emotional needs of the other. Spatial separation can amount to neglect; it can be experienced as rejection. Conversely, there may be insufficient separateness as in any relationship where one person controls or suffocates the other. The emotional needs of the person being possessed are often not recognized or attended to.

Frequently, therefore, it is an entirely new experience for a patient who comes into analysis (or into psychotherapy) to find that there can be space within an intimate relationship. And by 'space', here, I am referring in particular to the freedom *to think* whatever, *to feel* whatever, *to express* whatever, and *to be* whatever belongs to the patient's spontaneity in the session and to his/her autonomous being.

Different kinds of playing

There are two particular realms of experience in which we can find precursors to what may later be found in the analytic space: I am thinking of *the capacity to be alone in the presence of another person* (Winnicott 1965: ch. 2) and *playing*. These are closely related to each other, and I have tried to describe the interplay between them in my paper 'Samuel Beckett's relationship to his mother-tongue' (Casement 1982).

> [Beckett] had intimately known this strangulation of his creativity from which there was no way on but back. He could not write whilst there was no room for creative play, and yet it was particularly in the ability to play with words, and with language, that his genius ultimately lay.

> Let us examine this area of creativity [at the point of its first appearance]. To be free to enter into imaginative and creative play a child needs there to be a space between himself and the mother, over which he has the autonomous rights of initiative. Given this space, which Winnicott (1965: ch. 2) describes as 'being alone in the presence of the mother', the child begins to explore the creative potential of this space. But this requires of the mother a sensitive reluctance to enter into this play area uninvited. If all goes well the playing child can put into this the products of his own imagination – being free to 'include' her into, or out of, his play. He can use the mother's 'absent' presence or her 'present' absence as the warp and woof of his play. He can 'create' or 'uncreate' her at will, and thereby enjoy the magic of playing God and King over his own play-realm. The seeds of later creativity are sown and nurtured here.

> (Casement 1982: 38)

Much else is nurtured here, not least of which is the capacity to offer to others a similar freedom to become and be themselves. Some people, however, can only discover this through the realization that this being 'let be' had been missing for them in earlier life. Analysts in particular need to have, or need to develop, *a capacity to let the other person be.*

Unfortunately there are some parents who tend to take over their children's playing, which can result in a suppression of a child's natural spontaneity and capacity for imaginative play. Too many games, with rules invented by adults, can impair a child's development of autonomous playing. Of course there is a place for such adult-made games. But there is also a place for allowing a child to make up his/her own games without interference. For instance, a child left alone may use the counters for some board-game – like Monopoly – to create an imaginary family, school, or farmyard, the different counters being used to represent whatever belongs to the invented game. It is a great loss if an adult intervenes by prematurely trying to impose the 'rules' of the game, as if there were only one right way to play with a Monopoly set.

Creative play does not necessarily mean always playing alone; and this is the nature of an analysis when all is going well. In the first years this playing will often require the non-intrusive presence of a mother, or mother person, who is prepared to be included but equally prepared to be left out of her child's playing. The fact that she is not always included does not mean that her presence is not a necessary part of what is going on. It is often her background presence that provides the setting within which imaginative play can develop.

Example 10.1

A patient had been brought up by a mother who had frequently tried to control her play by providing whatever fitted in with the mother's idea of playing. When this patient herself became a mother she was careful not to impose a similar control upon her own child. Instead, she left toys and other objects around for her daughter to find, and to play with in her own way when she wished. Her baby soon developed a confidence in her own playing and she had very clear ideas about it.

When the grandmother was visiting, this baby (aged ten months) found her own imaginative play being interfered with:

the grandmother tried to take it over, as she used to do with her own children and other grandchildren. This grandchild, however, had her own ways of dealing with her. Whenever the grandmother handed a toy to be played with, which did not fit into the child's own play, this toy would be tossed aside as something for which she had no use at the time. The child would continue with her own play, cueing the grandmother to keep out of it. She would not include her in this playing.

The mother had been more able to allow her daughter the freedom for creative play. She was often used as a background presence, providing security but not always being included, whilst at other times her child would actively draw her into taking part. There was no compliant playing here!

There are lessons in this for the analyst. Patients need to be allowed the freedom to use the analytic space in their own way, not to have imposed upon them the analyst's preconceptions. For some patients it is especially important that the analyst can remain in the background – not having to be the focus all the time of something called transference – to be included by the patient or to be used as a background presence whilst the patient continues with his/her own thoughts, feelings, associations.[3] The timing and nature of interventions by the analyst is a skill that is always having to be attuned to the individual patient.

Monitoring the analytic space

The analytic space represents a freedom to work with the patient at understanding whatever he or she brings. But this freedom depends upon there still being a 'reflective viewpoint' within the analytic space, not entirely taken over by what is happening between analyst and patient, from which each can examine what has been going on between them.

The analyst needs to monitor regularly what is being put into the analytic space by him/herself, because whatever the analyst contributes to the interaction with the patient can either enhance the opportunities for analysing what is happening in the analytic relationship, or it can deflect from this and confuse attempts at analytic understanding.[4] Within limits, an analyst can allow him/herself to be drawn into different kinds of relating to the patient (see below). But if the analyst begins to behave in ways that are too much like key figures in the patient's past, it will become difficult for the patient to recognize any transference element that may be attached to that behaviour. The analytic space may then become lost – there being (at least temporarily) no 'reflective viewpoint' possible from which to analyse anything as transference or projection. That loss of analytic space occurs whenever there is too little difference between what is now coming from the analyst and how others have previously behaved towards the patient. No analysis is then possible until a sufficient difference has been re-established between the analyst's objective reality and whatever the patient may be putting on to the analyst (see Chapters 5 and 9).

The analytic process

What happens within the analytic space, when all goes well, is the product of the analytic process. A primary element in this process is the unconscious expression of internal conflict and feeling-states that have previously been repressed for lack of any other way to 'deal' with them. (This is a manifestation of unconscious hope; see Chapter 7.) However, contrary to the expectations of what common sense might suggest, the unconscious search here is not simply for better experience (see Chapters 5 and 6). It is for a sufficient security within which it may eventually come to feel safe enough for the patient to risk feeling again unsafe – in order to work through the feelings that had been associated with earlier difficult experiences. And whether that security can be found in the presence of the analyst will depend, to a large extent, on his/her ability to preserve the analytic space from the disturbances that can arise from the analyst's way of being with the patient.

When an analyst attempts to control the course of an analysis, the analytic space becomes constricted and the process is altered. What follows will then reflect the patient's responses to the analyst's influence. A lot may happen and changes ensue. However, changes that have been brought about under these conditions are not necessarily due to the analytic process: they may be more the product of an embattled relationship.

The analyst aims to be servant of the analytic process, not its master: firm when necessary, responsive to different kinds of need, but otherwise unobtrusive. The analyst's effectiveness is best demonstrated through learning to follow the analytic process, not in trying to control it. And when the analytic space is most clearly preserved for the patient, providing that unique opportunity for the patient to grow more fully into him/herself, the analytic process can be seen to have a life and direction of its own. Where it might lead cannot be anticipated, and what is then experienced by the patient goes far beyond the bounds of expectation.

The analyst's involvement with the patient's internal world

As we discover in the course of working analytically, all relating is mediated in some measure through the unconscious internal world of the patient by such processes as projection, projective identification, and transference. It is in order to identify most clearly the effects of these processes that the patient is given optimal freedom for these perceptual distortions to occur also within the analytic relationship.

It used to be suggested that the analyst should remain detached, an uninvolved observer and interpreter of the patient's transference as it unfolds. As I have already suggested (Chapter 8) it is now more widely recognized that the analyst, if he or she is not remaining defensively detached, will sooner or later become drawn into some interaction with the patient's internal drama, and this can be diagnostically useful. I believe that this level of response to the patient's unconscious is an essential part of the analytic process.

The technical point is that the analyst can allow him/herself, to a moderate degree, to become involved in the patient's psychic drama, as this emerges within the analytic relationship. I had provisionally called this 'diagnostic response' or diagnostic countertransference (Casement 1973), and in 1976 Sandler said:

> Parallel to the 'free-floating attention' of the analyst is what I should like to call his *free-floating responsiveness*. The analyst is, of course, not a machine in absolute self-control, only experiencing on the one hand, and delivering interpretations on the other, although much of the literature might seem to paint such a picture. Among many other things he talks, he greets the patient, he makes arrangements about practical matters, he may joke and, to some degree, allow his responses to depart from the classical psychoanalytic norm. My contention is that in the analyst's overt reactions to the patient as well as in his thoughts and feelings what can be called his 'role-responsiveness' shows itself, not only in his feelings but also in his attitudes and behaviour, as a crucial element in his 'useful' countertransference.
>
> (Sandler 1976: 45)

When the analyst is drawn into some re-enactment of the patient's internal drama different kinds of relating emerge. For instance, the analyst may become like one or other of the parents, or some other significant relationship, in ways that are typical of the patient's experience. It then becomes clearer what aspects of which object relationships are being relived. For this to be useful in the analysis, it is essential that the analyst also retain sufficient separateness from the interaction to be able to reflect upon it carefully before attempting to interpret (see Chapter 4). Otherwise there is a risk that the analyst may begin to 'act-in', which will disturb the analytic process, making it more difficult to see what, in the current interaction, belongs to the patient and what to the analyst. It is then not easy to make use of such moments in a way that can be helpful to the patient. But when the re-enactment is in response to the patient – and kept within careful limits – the cues to what is needed are often being supplied (unconsciously) by the patient.

Example 10.2

A patient (Miss R) had begun to talk more and more quietly in her sessions. I then had the problem of either continuing to point this out (at the risk of seeming to nag her, as I had already been asking her to speak up a bit) or trying to piece together as much as I could from what I was able to hear. Through listening in this way, I began to sense that there might be an important communication in the softness of her talking. As I could not hear her words, it was almost like having to listen to a pre-verbal child.

From the despairing tone of the patient's voice, I gradually formed the impression that she might be feeling hopeless because I was not understanding her. I then said to her: 'I think that there is something important about the way in which you are talking to me – talking so that I can hardly hear. I could, again, have asked you to speak louder. Instead, I have realized that I will only pick up what you are trying to get across to me if I listen very carefully, as a mother might with her infant who does not have any words. And what I am sensing is that you are feeling that I am not in touch with you. I believe that this is what you need me to understand, that I am not at this moment understanding you.'

The patient began to weep. When she was able to speak again she said: 'But you understood that you did not understand.

That is what makes the difference.'

From this brief but important experience, Miss R began to realize that her parents had seldom recognized when they had not been understanding her. They had too often assumed that they 'knew'. This realization was painful for her – the 'pain of contrast'. (This was all the more painful for Miss R as she was still working through the loss of her earlier idealization of her parents, in particular that of her father.)

At different stages in an analysis the analyst is likely to be drawn into representing a wide range of 'parental functions' – from that of the mother, who is drawn into a near-symbiotic closeness to her infant, to that of the father who needs to provide firmness and structure if the growing child is not to remain caught up in that earlier tie to the mother.

The analyst does not attempt *actively* to fulfil any of those parental functions. But, in my opinion, the analyst should not hold back from being used by the patient to represent them. And I would include here the mirroring function of the parent who is needed by the child for affirmation.

Diverse theories: diverse applications

The diversity of human experience defies definition, though the desire to demonstrate the notion that psychoanalysis is a science has tempted some analysts to offer definitive explanations of human interaction. There is an inescapable conflict in this. On the one hand, we need to be familiar with whatever can be established as common clinical experience: without a sufficient framework, we would be relying too much upon guesswork and intuition. On the other hand, we are constantly being challenged to discover what else may apply better to the individual patient. Because the diversity of human interaction goes so far beyond the strictures of any science, what we do as analysts will not always be manifestly consistent or without its contradictions.[5]

Different patients need different approaches. Most patients at some time need firmness, to provide containment for states that are chaotic or which threaten to get out of control. But also, many at some time need to feel that they are with an analyst who can offer an exploratory space within which the patient's own individuality and creativity can develop more fully. Analysts therefore need to acquire the capacity to work in different ways at different times.

I also think that it is salutary to remember that each school of psychoanalysis has been developed over years, from clinical experience viewed in different ways. Different schools have come into being (as with schismatic groups in religion) through a recognition that there had been some serious omission, or over-emphasis, in the thinking of other schools. The part-truth newly highlighted by fresh thinking all too often comes to be elevated as being *the truth*, at which point this new position also begins to qualify for criticism and correction by others. In human affairs there cannot be any one view that excludes all others.[6]

The proponents of various analytic theories, and the different techniques that have evolved around them, often vie with each other as if one school of psychoanalysis were right and the others therefore wrong. What is overlooked in this rivalry is the degree to which individual analysts are drawn to theoretical and technical positions that *fit their own personalities*. Inevitably, analysts will themselves have been more helped by some theories than by others. It is natural that they will more readily see their patients in terms of those particular theories and the issues pertaining to them. Also, to some extent all analysts are influenced, in the way that they work, by the nature of their own personalities. Thus, the aggressive person may become a belligerent analyst, the insecure either dogmatic or passive, the indecisive exaggeratedly open-minded, the narcissistic too often insistent that they must be right, and so on. I believe that the personal contribution to styles of working is not recognized often enough for what it is and dealt with in the training analysis or, later, by means of self-analysis.

It is not just a matter of different styles that is needed: the analyst may also need to draw upon a range of different theories, to encompass the diversity of clinical phenomena that will be encountered. For example: the nature of many patients' problems still requires the analyst to draw especially upon Freud's theories of libido and theories of conflict. The problems of others, however, are so clearly related to early environmental failure that the analyst will be better helped by the theories of other writers such as Winnicott. With yet other patients, the analyst needs to be familiar with Kleinian contributions to our understanding of such phenomena as the dynamics of destructive narcissism. With others, again, the analyst will need to understand the search for ameliorative self-experience and may be better helped by ideas drawn from Kohut's self psychology.[7]

In my opinion, therefore, analysts cannot afford to be too monogamously wedded to one particular theory. They will be better helped in their clinical work if they are willing to learn even from analysts whose theories and technique are quite at variance with their own. The reluctance to do this is understandable. But without this inter-group learning there is a tendency for positions on theory and technique to become fossilized, with opportunities for creative interchange lost in the process of sterile rivalry.[8]

Important clinical opportunities are also missed if there is too fixed an adherence either to a technical position which stresses the malignancy of the patient's pathology, or to one that overstates the benign nature of the unconscious. Because of the diversity of the unconscious, in which contradictions can co-exist, we have to tolerate the discovery that logically opposite formulations can each, at different times, be true. Much discord between different theoretical positions may have grown out of an inability to face this clinical fact. Human truth cannot be unified. At times it requires paradox to contain it. And the patient will not necessarily be confused, as some people assume, in the face of different bodies of theory. When an analyst discovers insight *alongside* the patient, and does not impose it dogmatically, a process of synthesis takes place within the patient, from which a coherent understanding gradually emerges, based upon those insights that have most helped to make sense of the patient's experience.

Different approaches to psychic depth: the psychotic experience in analysis

One crucial difference in technique distinguishes those who attempt to control the analytic process from those who attempt to follow it. These represent very different schools of thought about the 'correct' approach to the deep unconscious.

One approach is to proceed from surface to depth – analysing defence and resistance before content, ego before id. The rationale is that defences have been necessary to the patient, so that 'The analyst's interventions should aim at making the patient's reasonable ego better able to cope with the old danger situations' (Greenson 1967: 138).

The Kleinian approach, on the other hand, is to interpret the deepest anxiety immediately:

My view, based on empiric observation, [is] that the analyst should not shy away from making a deep interpretation even at the start of the analysis, since the material belonging to a deeper layer of the mind will come back again later and be worked through. As I have said before, the function of deep-going interpretation is simply to open the door to the unconscious, to diminish the anxiety that has been stirred up and thus to prepare the way for analytic work.

(Klein 1932: 24)

For Kleinian analysts, therefore, the focus for an interpretation is aimed at the point of greatest urgency – the most immediate anxiety. But how that point of urgency is identified can be assessed in various ways by different analysts.

The implications of interpretive activity

Different consequences follow from contrasting views of the analytic process and space, and these are demonstrated in the different levels of interpretive activity that reflect each view.

There are analysts who regard the dynamics of the patient's unconscious as potentially so destructive that they think they must always be in control of the analytic process. The result is often that the analyst is very active, and I think that the patient's responses to that activity often reflect the disturbing quality of these attempts to control everything that happens in the analytic space. It is debatable how much of the paranoid material that emerges in the course of such an analysis is necessarily a primary expression of the patient's internal world: *some* of it at least is likely to be in response to the analyst's manner of working.

Once the analyst departs from sparing, provisional interpretations, he not only disturbs the listening situation but has made it difficult to re-establish it. He ought therefore to make up his mind beforehand what policy he is going to pursue.

(Glover 1955: 96)

There is still a lot to be learned about how best to preserve the analytic space so that the analytic process can freely unfold. This is what I was intuitively trying to do in my work with Joy (Chapter 3) and more consciously ever since. It has been my experience that, though I do not actively search for the psychotic areas in a patient's personality, but address myself to whatever is emerging in the course of an analysis, patients eventually feel safe enough to bring their hidden psychotic states into the analysis. An important element in this development is the gradual building of trust during the analytic work that has gone before. This allows a patient to 'abandon' that trust for a while and to enter into a state that may, intermittently, become deeply distrusting. However, the basic trust that had been built up before is not necessarily destroyed or completely lost. Instead, it seems to be relegated to a background position, to the working alliance. Sometimes, even that may seem to be in abeyance but, nevertheless, it is not altogether absent.

It is within this context, of allowing the analytic process to unfold in its own way, that a patient can feel safe enough to risk feeling psychotically unsafe within the analytic relationship. I therefore believe that, when sufficient time has been given (or has been possible) for establishing a background of trust, the timing of this emergence of psychotic states in the analysis reflects the patient's readiness for this and is a true expression of the analytic process.[9]

When a patient is manifestly psychotic it frequently requires extraordinary skill and mental agility to contain what has become uncontained. Therefore, when an analyst *goes* for the psychotic depth, I think that there may be some patients who feel stripped of the defences that had been needed to keep psychotic areas contained. The result may then be that virulent psychotic states break out, as if to punish the analyst who has removed that defensive containment. Perhaps the patient is also challenging the analyst to take over total management of his/her unconscious, when the analyst has acted as if everything about the patient's thinking were within the analyst's competence to know and to control. Could it be, I have wondered, that some of the florid part-object material that seems typical of some analyses is the result of too much having been released from the unconscious too quickly? And may this kind of experience contribute to the view that some analysts seem to have of their patients – as if they were always dealing with such malignant forces in the unconscious that they do not feel able to recognize anything in the patient's deep unconscious that they can safely trust?

Every patient has some psychotic areas and these do usually come into an analysis sooner or later, if they are not deflected by the analyst. But I do not, personally, 'go' for these depths. Instead, I try to make it possible for them to emerge more safely in the patient's own time, when sufficient ego strengths have been developed for the patient to be able to tolerate that experience. This may explain why I do not so often encounter fragmentation of the ego to quite the same degree as we find in some clinical accounts from analysts who work differently.

An issue of technique here is that, for mental and emotional space to exist between people, there have to be boundaries to the personality of each. When a patient's ego is unable to maintain these boundaries, the analytic space becomes at times invaded by 'bizarre contents', resulting from the processes of splitting and projection taking place in the patient's mind. Analysts, therefore, have to be able to 'field' these projections (or transferences) as best they can, to understand them and the dynamics behind them. But the degree of interpretive activity which may then seem to be necessary can also invade the analytic space. That is why I believe that it is preferable for analysts to meet whatever emerges from the patient's unconscious, with the firmness appropriate to contain it, rather than to get into the patient's mind in an anticipatory way. The attempt at analysing what emerges from the patient's mind gets complicated if it arises largely in response to the analyst's ways of interpreting. And it is even more confusing for patients if they are then expected to own such responses as if they were originating, unprovoked, solely from within themselves.

Profound experience

As indicated in Chapter 6, the gains in analysis are by no means limited to insight or to those changes that follow from interpreting the transference. There are times when significant change takes place around an experience that can be regarded as 'profound' even if not specifically an experience of the transference. For instance, a patient can be profoundly affected by experiencing something quite new in the analysis, or by re-experiencing something that had been 'forgotten' and lost. Unlike other profound experiences, which may be encountered in solitude, this always involves both participants in the analytic relationship.

Example 10.3

Mrs S (aged 44) was a patient who had remained hidden for most of her life behind a facade of false-self compliance. She did what was expected of her, fearing that if she did not she would be rejected.

> One day Mrs S said to me: 'You sometimes try too hard to understand me.' This prompted me to realize that there was something else that she needed from me, but it was not yet clear what this was. A few weeks later she came very

punctually to a session but she did not speak. For the whole session she remained silent. During this time I was wondering what to make of this. Was she resisting? (The atmosphere did not feel combative.) Was she needing me to reach out to her, to help her out of the silence? (She showed no signs of tension or anxiety.) Was she distressed, needing me to be aware of that? (There was a sense of calm and peacefulness in the session – no sense of distress.) I then felt that she needed me just to *let her be*.

Towards the end of the session I began to wonder how to deal with the ending. If I said nothing this could be unhelpfully ambiguous. It could be misunderstood as retaliatory. And, if the experience had been as I was now sensing, it would have been a pity to have spoiled that by leaving the patient with an uncertainty as to how I had understood it. I therefore said: 'I have not felt that there was any need for me to speak in this session. But, before we end for today, it might help if I tell you where I have been in the silence. I have been remembering the time, a few weeks ago, when you told me that I had been trying too hard to understand.' After a pause the patient got up to leave, and at the door she said: 'Thank you.'

The next day Mrs S lay in silence with the same atmosphere of calm. Throughout the session she said nothing and neither did I. There was no need now, I felt, to explain where I was in this further silence. At the end she got up to leave and, once again, she said: 'Thank you.' And the day following Mrs S said to me: 'I want to thank you for not speaking. I felt more real in those last two sessions than I have ever felt before. *You allowed me to BE.*'

This experience, although profound, could not alone change this patient's life. But it could serve as a touchstone-experience, by which she began to recognize the difference between feeling real and being compliant. It could act as a pointer for the realness she still needed to find in herself.

Example 10.4

Since he had begun to go to school, Mr T (aged 29) had been crippled by the neurotic conversion of difficult feelings into a compelling need to go frequently to the toilet. There, in the form of faeces, he would symbolically get rid of his feelings, safely into the toilet.

Mr T had learned from his mother that she could not bear to be confronted by any distress of his. He had therefore developed ways in which he could keep his mother from breaking down, even keep her alive, by taking care that he never expressed to her any feelings that she might not be able to cope with. *He* mothered *her*. In particular Mr T could not express anger. I therefore began to feel sure that this patient had never been able to communicate through projective identification (getting his mother to feel what he could not manage on his own), and these feelings had come to be regarded by him as for ever unmanageable, even lethal.

> In one session Mr T emphasized that it was largely to avoid humiliation that he had to go so frequently to the toilet. In association to this, he added that he felt sure that if he did ever express really what he felt he would be humiliated for that too. He was also afraid that I did not realize what I was asking of him when I spoke as if he might become able to show me more directly what he was feeling. He felt sure that I would retaliate if he did, like his parents. His mother could not bear to be confronted with what he was feeling, neither could his father.

> I replied that he seemed to see me as a sadistic surgeon who, when lancing a boil, would blame the patient for the mess that emerged. I added that he seemed to have no sense that a surgeon who knows his business would also take care of the mess, as part of enabling the boil to discharge its poison. Mr T retorted that it was easy for me to say that: 'But it's just words.'

I reflected upon this response and realized that I had used this analogy before – with another patient some years ago. It was not new, so I could readily see how it might sound like 'just words'. Also, I had thought first of an analogy that was surgical and therefore distant. From this internal supervision a quite different image came into my mind.

> I then said: 'Another image has now come to me, and I am not going to bother whether it could be medically correct: I shall use it just as it comes to me. I see a mother holding her sick child on her lap. The child has an obstruction of the bowel from which the child will die if it cannot be relieved of this. But the mother senses that, if she can hold her child securely enough, he may be able to let this go and he will not die. I can

then imagine the mother's tears of relief upon finding that her child's bowel has functioned again as it should. She will not give a thought to the mess this might have created in her lap, for the joy of knowing that her child will not die.'

Mr T followed this description in silence, obviously moved. When I had finished speaking I noticed that he was silently crying. This was something quite new in his analysis.

After a period of quiet reflection Mr T said: 'For the first time I can see the possibility that there can be some hope that I could become freed of my symptoms. Until now I have really just been going through the motions of analysis, not really believing that it could make any difference at all.'

This was merely the beginning of a beginning. But, from that day, Mr T began to discover that he did not still have to protect me from his feelings by going to the toilet several times on most days before coming to his sessions. Instead, he began to bring his feelings to me more directly. At first he could usually tell me only about what he had been feeling before he came. Gradually, however, he began to express his feelings as he experienced them in the session: they did not have to be converted into symptoms and 'got rid of' down toilets. Rather, a person could be available to him to receive whatever he was feeling and to help him with that. This was an entirely new discovery. It was a truly profound and transformative experience.

Mr T also began to discover that the analytic space was there specifically for him, and it was provided by a person. Into this space he now began to be able to express his own most dreaded feelings; and within this space he could find a *personal* containment which began to change his experience of them. His feelings could become, once again, a communication of distress in search of a personal response – with a renewed hope of finding it.

When such changes occur in an analysis the implications can be far reaching, even to the point of changing a person's life. Some patients communicate and relate in new ways; their view of themselves and of others changes radically; the sense that feelings are dangerous gives way when they discover that another person has after all been containing and managing them so that the former view of these feelings (as unmanageable) does not have to dominate the rest of life. Without that beginning there can be no growth. But when the process of growth is renewed it can continue.

Conclusion

In this book and its predecessor I have described some of my own clinical explorations and my wondering about the processes involved in the analytic encounter.

During this quest, I have had to recognize (like a climber) the limits of my own competence – to know when I must follow a guide or to stay on the 'beaten track'. And whilst I have been exploring away from the more usual routes, I have always sensed the need still to be held by the life-lines of classical theory and technique, to save me from falling or to help me find my way back when I have begun to get lost.

Inevitably, in the course of my journey I have made my share of mistakes, learning from which has always been important: but along the way I have also had many surprises. I have found much that has confirmed what I had previously accepted only provisionally (and reluctantly) upon the authority of others.

The analytic journey is often difficult and painful for analyst as well as patient, quite frequently bewildering, and at times awesome. Progress is slow and sometimes intermittent. Nevertheless, working with the analytic process can at the same time be extraordinarily enriching (to both participants) as true aliveness is rediscovered, as creativity is released from what had been blocking it, and as patients recover the capacity to be more fully themselves and to be playful.

The question

Will you, sometime, who have sought so long and seek
Still in the slowly darkening hunting ground,
Catch sight some ordinary month or week
Of that strange quarry you scarcely thought you sought –
Yourself, the gatherer gathered, the finder found,
The buyer, who would buy all, in bounty bought –
And perch in pride on the princely hand, at home,
And there, the long hunt over, rest and roam?

(Edwin Muir 1984: 122)

Notes

Chapter 1

1 This chapter is a revised version of a paper that was originally entitled 'Between the lines: *On Learning from the Patient* – before and after', previously published in The *British Journal of Psychotherapy* 4: 86-93 (1987).

2 Projective identification is a term first used by Melanie Klein (1946) to describe a process whereby parts of the ego are thought of as forced into another person who is then expected to become identified with whatever has been projected. I have given a brief outline of the different aspects of projective identification elsewhere (Casement 1985: 100, note 3). A fuller description of projective identification, along with all the relevant references, may be found in *A Dictionary of Kleinian Thought* (Hinshelwood 1989: 179-208).

3 See Winnicott's 'spatula game' (1958: Chapters 3 and 4; 1989: Chapter 40).

4 I am a member of the Independent Analysts' Group of the British Psycho-Analytical Society, as distinct from the Kleinians and what are now called the Contemporary Freudians.

Chapter 2

1 An earlier version of this chapter was presented as a paper at the British Association of Psychotherapists' Annual Conference, November 1985. It was also presented to numerous meetings of psychotherapists, and psychotherapy training associations, in and around London. It has been previously published in *Free Associations* 5: 90-104 (1986); also in *The Bulletin of the British Association of Psychotherapists* 17: 3-16 (1986).

2 What I am describing as a 'transferential attitude' to elements of the clinical situation is not transference in the classical sense – nor is it truly countertransference. It does, however, have some similarity to the definition of countertransference as the analyst's transference towards the patient (Reich 1951; Gitelson 1952). Reich says of this: 'In such cases the patient represents for the analyst an object of the past on to whom past feelings and wishes are projected' (1951: 26).

What is transferred in the transferential attitude is, of course, not a past object relationship: it is the understanding of some other clinical experience which is attributed to present clinical phenomena. The sense of similarity triggers a transferential attitude, just as transference too is triggered by some element of similarity which is treated as sameness.

3 This example is described more fully elsewhere (Casement 1985: 20-1).

4 I have discussed this case more fully elsewhere (Casement 1985: 89-92 and 135-7).

5 The notion of 'double-bind' was first suggested by Bateson *et al.* (1956). It is used to describe a situation in which contradictory demands are being put upon a child (or patient, see Laing 1961) in such a way that there is no avenue of escape or challenge. (See also Rycroft 1968.)

Chapter 3

1 Dilys Daws, a child psychotherapist, said of this clinical sequence:

The problem between Joy and her mother is not just that Joy is *not* a boy, but that she *is* a girl. As you point out, some of her exploration is to find her female genitals, as something positive, not just as lack of penis. However I think this is part of her problem, i.e. that she is the *same* as her mother with all the identification/rivalry issues that ensue.

I cannot know, but would guess that her mother had a serious postnatal depression after Joy's birth, triggered by Joy being a girl. The lack of contact between them (which was not the case with the boys) may be the result of such a period, which makes it difficult for a mother to pick up cues from the baby and to respond to them. If there was such a period, and it was because Joy was a girl and not because of some other factor, then this might have been stirred up by the mother possibly having had a difficult relationship with her own mother, and the birth of a daughter facing her with having to deal with a mother–daughter relationship all over again. (Difficult births can also stir up the same sequence of postnatal trauma and a problem in making contact with the new baby.) Both mother and Joy may have felt that life would be much simpler if all these issues could be avoided by a preference for boys and penises! I think there are hints of all this from session 16 onwards.

(Dily Daws: personal correspondence)

I think that this hypothetical view offers a most plausible background for the relationship between Joy and her mother. My difficulty at the time was that I was not given proper referral information for psychotherapy with this child; and having been given the mixed brief that I was, to be a reading teacher 'with an eye to the therapeutic need', I was hardly in a position to find out such personal details from the mother. And now, these many years later, I think it would be improper to ask.

Further detail on the effects of postnatal depression upon the subsequent relationship between mother and infant can be found in *Through the Night* (Daws 1989: ch. 13).

Chapter 4

1 This chapter is based upon a paper that was written by invitation, and published in *Contemporary Psychoanalysis* 22: 548-59 (1986). An earlier version was presented to the British Society of Analytical Psychology, London, December 1985; and subsequently to the British Psycho-Analytical Society, May 1986.

2 Bollas has given other cautions about the use of countertransference in interpretation; they are complementary to mine.

> As in any analytic intervention, it is exceedingly important to consider whether the patient can use an intervention, and this is why I place so much emphasis on the gradual presentation over time of the analyst's sense of the situation, as a prerequisite to any direct expression of the countertransference. Any disclosure on the analyst's part of how he feels must be experienced by the patient as a legitimate and natural part of the analytic process. If it comes as a shock, then the analyst has failed in his technique. . . . There are some patients to whom one could not ever usefully express one's experience as their object, and this must be accepted.
>
> (Bollas 1987: 210-11)

3 When I originally wrote the paper on which this chapter is based I was not familiar with the papers by Tansey and Burke (1985) and Burke and Tansey (1985), which are complementary to this chapter and offer interesting parallels. (See also Samuels 1985: 185-7; 1989: ch. 9.) .

Chapter 5

1 The original version of this chapter was written, at the invitation of the editor of Free Association Books, as one of the papers to be published in memory of Dr John Klauber, whose Freud Memorial Lectures (written just before his death) were the basis and inspiration of the book in which these papers were then published: *Illusion and Spontaneity*, ed. R. Young, London: Free Association Books (1987).

2 Klaus Fink has given us a most useful summary of Matte Blanco's theory in his paper 'From symmetry to asymmetry' (Fink 1989), in which he summarizes the principles of 'generalization' and 'symmetry' that Matte Blanco has described, from which it follows that there is in the unconscious no distinction between past, present, and future; and the part is experienced as identical to the whole (see Matte Blanco 1975: 38-9 and 137-40).

Fink adds his own comments in relation to trauma:

> In the thought system of symmetry, time does not exist. An event
> that occurred yesterday can also occur today or tomorrow. . . .
> This means that, for instance, traumatic events of the past are not
> only seen in the unconscious as ever present and permanently
> happening but also about to happen, hence the need or compulsion
> to repeat the defensive behaviour (Freud, 1914).
>
> (Fink 1989: 482-3)

And later he says:

> The whole object and its parts are equivalent and exchangeable
> because any part of an object represents the whole object and the
> whole object may represent any of its parts.
>
> (Fink 1989: 483)

When we relate these thoughts to traumatic experience we can understand better why it is that a patient feels alerted by any similarity to
part of that experience, and why something that has happened in the
past can feel as if it is still about to happen.

3 I focus in proper detail on the issue of corrective emotional
experience in the next chapter.

Chapter 6

1 An earlier version of this chapter was written by invitation for a
special issue devoted to the theme of 'The corrective emotional
experience re-visited' (*Psychoanalytic Inquiry* 10: 325–46, 1990).
2 Winnicott's handling of severe regression is illustrated in Margaret
Little's accounts of her analysis with him (Little 1985; 1987).
3 It is also important not to make the opposite mistake, that of
thinking of the patient as only an adult. Terrible misunderstandings
can follow, as Jung demonstrated in his reaction to a patient who had
dreamed of 'an idiot child of about two years old. It was sitting on a
chamber pot and had smeared itself with faeces'. In his analysis of
that dream, Jung says:

> In small children, such uncouth behaviour is somewhat unusual,
> but still possible. They may be intrigued by their faeces, which are
> coloured and have an odd smell. . . . But the dreamer, the doctor,
> was no child; he was a grown man. And therefore the dream image
> . . . is a sinister symbol. When he told me the dream, I realised
> that his normality was a compensation. I had caught him in the
> nick of time, for the latent psychosis was within a hair breadth of
> breaking out and becoming manifest.
>
> (Jung 1967: 157-8)

Jung concluded from this that he should stop treating this patient.
This account is, of course, from a long time ago. But I am told that
some psychotherapy students still quote this example as justifying a

retreat from regressive material presented by a patient. When a patient begins to trust the analyst or therapist it will be just such disturbing aspects of the internal world that will be presented for understanding – not for a panic retreat by the therapist!

4 I realize that I am describing a view here that may be close to that of self psychology, but it has been arrived at independently.

5 See 'Afterthought' at the end of this chapter for a consideration of what the consequences may be for the patient if the analyst has not had this kind of experience in his/her training analysis.

6 A major difference, in the experience of trainee patients, is that the ending of analysis/therapy is much more final for most patients than for those who go on to practise – joining a group of like-minded colleagues (which often includes the former training analyst). This continued (but often indirect) association with the former analyst/therapist can mask a continuing dependence and the sustaining of change by means of that association. The irony is that few analysts or therapists are faced so starkly with an ending as most other patients are. This raises important questions about their sensitivity to the issues involved in ending and their competence to deal with these fully enough with those patients who will not be going on to train.

7 Other therapeutic factors not mentioned here are stressed by a number of other authors, quite apart from mutative transference interpretations as described by Strachey (1934). In particular I wish to draw attention to Blum's paper 'The position and value of extratransference interpretation' (1983), Symington's paper 'The analyst's act of freedom as agent of therapeutic change' (1983) and that of Stewart 'Interpretation and other agents for psychic change' (1990).

8 In my chapter 'Analytic holding under pressure' (1985: ch. 7) I give details of a case that is also discussed in *example 5.7* of this volume. I describe there how a patient unconsciously prompted me to let her use me in the transference to represent her mother who had fainted at a most crucial moment in her early childhood. The patient could then work through, in relation to me, the terror and rage that had belonged to that experience.

9 My comments here about the use of words need to be read alongside Freud's *Appendix* 'Words and things' (Freud 1915: 209-15) and other statements on this subject such as the papers by Olinick (1982), O'Shaughnessy (1983), and Tuckett (1983), for example.

10 Rycroft has some important observations to make on the subject of interpretation in his papers 'The nature and function of the analyst's communication to the patient' and 'An enquiry into the function of words in the psychoanalytical situation' (Rycroft 1968: chs. 5 and 6).

11 There are a number of authors that I have not quoted here who also address the issues raised in this chapter. I am thinking in particular of Balint (1952, 1968), Kohut (1984), and Bowlby (1988) to name but a few. I also wish to highlight one other (J. Klein 1988) who gives us a valuable exploration of the literature along with her own contributions on this subject.

What I have given here are my own observations, drawn from clinical experience, which I offer in parallel to the findings of others. It is my hope that some validation of what other practitioners have observed may arise from a comparison of these parallels.

Chapter 7

1 An earlier version of this chapter was presented to a meeting of the Independent Analysts' Group of the British Psycho-Analytical Society, October 1987; and subsequently at the Annual Training and Development Conference 'Connections and Boundaries: Interfacing Traditional and Humanistic Psychotherapy' organized by the Association of Humanistic Psychology Practitioners, at Hawkwood College, Stroud, November 1987. It was also given (at the invitation of the Swedish Mental Health Association) as 'The Scandinavian Lecture' in Stockholm, March 1988; and in Athens, May 1989, as a public lecture organized by the Hellenic Society of Psychoanalytic Psychotherapy. It has now been published (in Greek) in *Psychologika Themata* 2: 100–11 (Athens 1989).
2 The only reference to 'Hope' that I could initially find in the psychoanalytic journals familiar to me was the paper 'On hope: its nature and psychotherapy' (Boris 1976). That author had also noticed its absence in the literature:

> If one searches the standard psychoanalytic literature (I have in mind, for instance, Freud, A. Freud, Fenichel, Fairbairn, H. Segal) one is apt to find little in the index between 'homosexuality' and 'hysteria', save 'hunger'. 'Hope' itself is nowhere to be seen.
>
> (Boris 1976: 139)

Since then the following paper has appeared, 'Hope and hopelessness: a technical problem?' (Mehler and Argentieri 1989).
3 If during an ongoing analysis or therapy it seems to be in the patient's best interests for him/her to be referred elsewhere, no action on this should be instigated except after the most careful examination of what a patient may be presenting for attention at such times of crisis and whether this could yet be managed without terminating treatment with that patient. It should also be clearly understood that, when treatment is prematurely ended, this is a treatment failure – not necessarily a fault of the patient. Nevertheless, every patient who is passed on will take this rejection as the latest of many, and (often) as evidence of some dreadful truth about themselves that is assumed to be hidden behind whatever reasons are given for that treatment decision.

Chapter 8

1 An earlier version of this chapter was presented at a Conference on 'The Inter-relation of Inner World and the Environment: Problems of

Interpretation in Clinical Work' held at University College, London, September 1988.

2 I did not then (in the 1970s) forbid patients to smoke in sessions. Instead, I would occasionally invite a patient to explore the reasons for wanting to smoke *just then*. At this stage in Miss M's analysis I felt it would have been counter-productive had I tried to control her smoking, even if 'only' by interpretation. She later gave up smoking quite spontaneously when she discovered that she no longer needed to turn to substitutes. That change, when it came, was truly autonomous; it was not compliant.

3 This is similar to the severity of superego found in the psychopath (Symington 1980).

4 Rosenfeld has given some important examples of impasse in analysis which clearly illustrate the analyst's contributions to this (Rosenfeld 1987).

Chapter 9

1 A somewhat different paper, but with the same title as that of this chapter, was presented to the British Society of Analytical Psychology, London, December 1985. The clinical substance of that earlier paper is now presented in Chapter 4.

2 In Chapter 2 I have already given an example of a patient who experienced her psychiatrist as behaving sexually towards her because of his frequent interpretation of Oedipal themes which she had also found exciting.

Chapter 10

1 Unfortunately, there are other forms of *bullying the patient* to be found in some descriptions of analysis. Most common (perhaps) is that of the attacking style of interpreting, usually rationalized as being aimed at 'getting through defences' or 'dealing with resistance'. This is particularly evident in some of the accounts of clinical work with narcissistic patients. The problem then is that this style of interpreting can too closely parallel the pathogenic behaviour of primary figures in the patient's formative life, against which behaviour the narcissistic defences had been formed in the first place. This parallel, in the analyst's manner of working with such patients, can often result in an impasse or breakdown in the analysis; or it may lead to an idealization of the 'strong' analyst and an identification with the aggressor. When this style of analysing is encountered in the course of a training analysis, some victims of that identification will be found amongst the next generation of patients. I believe that there may be a divergent 'strain' of analytic experience that is passed on in this way.

2 I am not advocating any notion of unlimited freedom for a child to have its own way. A child who is not given appropriate limits goes in search of them (see Chapter 3). It is in growing into a confident sense

of Self that a child most needs to be 'let be'. Libidinal demands are another matter altogether (see Chapter 6).

3 I think of this as similar to the two uses of the spatula: (a) to be shoved down patients' throats – as in repeated transference interpretations; and (b) to be found and to be played with – as in Winnicott's child consultations (see Chapter 1).

4 The point of the exercises in the last chapter was largely in order to highlight these interferences in the analytic space and process. Trial-identifying with the patient can always provide some help in preserving the analytic space, or in restoring it when it has become impaired.

5 In my opinion, psychoanalysis is not a science. But, as far as can be compatible with the individuality of each patient, it is quite proper that analysts should try to be 'scientific' in trying to establish the comparability between similar clinical situations. But, when the scientific attitude is taken too far – to establish the 'repeatability' that is a keystone to any science – the result can be interpretive work that becomes repetitive. It is then more likely to shape the process between patient and analyst rather than to follow it. I do not regard that as working in a truly psychoanalytic way.

6 I find it encouraging that Sandler suggests a similar openness to theories that relate more clearly to the clinical work in hand, rather than remaining chronically attached to a particular theoretical position. In his paper 'Reflections on some relations between psychoanalytic concepts and psychoanalytic practice' he says:

> If we abandon our search for the pot of theoretical gold at the end of the rainbow, then we may perhaps allow ourselves a greater degree of tolerance of concepts which are unclear and ill-defined, particularly those which have been created by people who have a different psychoanalytic background. . . .

> To try to satisfy all 'explanatory intents' with one comprehensive theory is clearly impossible, and I would urge the view that we have *a body of ideas*, rather than a consistent whole, that constitutes psychoanalytic theory. What is critical is not what psychoanalytic theory *should* be, but what should be *emphasized* within the whole compass of psychoanalytic thinking. *And what should be emphasized is that which relates to the work we have to do*. This means that for most of us the theory needs to be a clinically, psychopathologically and technically oriented one, which also includes a central preoccupation, not only with the abnormal, but with the normal as well.
>
> (Sandler 1983: 37)

7 Valuable over-views of these various theories can be found in Greenberg and Mitchell (1983) and in J. Klein (1988). Bollas has also expressed some interesting views on these issues (Bollas 1989: ch.5).

8 The opportunity that is missed, for a creative interchange of ideas

about clinical practice, is often illustrated when analysts of different persuasions respond to the presentation of a clinical paper. There are two particular trends noticeable in the discussion that follows. One approach to a paper, from a colleague who works differently, may be characterized by such a question as: 'What can I learn from this other view?' A creative dialogue may then follow. Often, however, the question seems to be: 'What can I find, in the view expressed in this paper, that I can use to justify *not learning anything from it*?' The aim then seems to be to prove that the speaker had been wrong, leaving the respondent with his/her own practice undisturbed.

9 I have described some of my work with one such patient elsewhere (Casement 1985: 147-52).

References

Alexander, F. (1954) 'Some quantitative aspects of psychoanalytic technique', *Journal of the American Psychoanalytic Association* 2: 685–701.

Alexander, F., French, T.M. *et al.* (1946) *Psychoanalytic Therapy: Principles and Application*, New York: Ronald Press.

Balint, M. (1952) *Primary Love and Psycho-Analytic Technique*, London: Tavistock.

—— (1968) *The Basic Fault*, London: Tavistock.

Bateson, G. *et al.* (1956) 'Toward a theory of schizophrenia', *Behavioral Science* 1: 251–64.

Bion, W.R. (1962) *Learning from Experience* in *Seven Servants*, New York: Aronson, 1977.

—— (1967a) 'Notes on memory and desire', *Psychoanalytic Forum* 2: 271–80; also in *Melanie Klein Today*, Volume 2, London: Routledge, 1988.

—— (1967b) *Second Thoughts*, New York: Aronson.

—— (1970) *Attention and Interpretation* in *Seven Servants*, New York: Aronson, 1977.

—— (1975) *Brazilian Lectures 2*, Rio de Janeiro: Imago Editora.

Blum, H.P. (1983) 'The position and value of extratransference interpretation', *Journal of the American Psychoanalytic Association* 31: 587–617.

Bollas, C. (1987) *The Shadow of the Object: Psychoanalysis of the Unthought Known*, London: Free Association Books.

—— (1989) *Forces of Destiny: Psychoanalysis and Human Idiom*, London: Free Association Books.

Boris, H.N. (1976) 'On hope: its nature and psychotherapy', *International Review of Psycho-Analysis* 3: 139–50.

Bowlby, J. (1988) *A Secure Base*, London: Routledge.

Burke, W.F. and Tansey, M.J. (1985) 'Projective identification and countertransference turmoil', *Contemporary Psychoanalysis* 21: 372–402.

Casement, P.J. (1963) 'The paradox of unity', *Prism* 69: 8–11.

—— (1964) 'False security?', *Prism* 88: 28–30.

—— (1969) 'The setting of limits: a belief in growth', *Case Conference*

16: 267–71; also in *The Voice of the Social Worker*, London: Bookstall Publications, 1970.

—— (1973) 'The supervisory viewpoint', in W.F. Finn (ed.) *Family Therapy in Social Work: Conference Papers*, London: Family Welfare Association.

—— (1982) 'Samuel Beckett's relationship to his mother-tongue', *International Review of Psycho-Analysis* 9: 35–44.

—— (1985) *On Learning from the Patient*, London: Tavistock.

Daws, D. (1989) *Through the Night*, London: Free Association Books.

Eliot, T.S. (1935) *Four Quartets*, London: Faber & Faber, 1949.

Fink, K. (1989) 'From symmetry to asymmetry', *International Journal of Psycho-Analysis* 70: 481–9.

Freud, S. (1909) 'Notes upon a case of obsessional neurosis', SE 10: 153–320. (*Standard Edition of the Complete Psychological Works of Sigmund Freud*, London: Hogarth Press, 1950–1974.)

—— (1914) 'Remembering, repeating and working-through', SE 12: 145–56.

—— (1915) 'The unconscious', SE 14: 159–215.

Gill, M.M. (1982) *Analysis of the Transference*, vol. 1, New York: International Universities Press.

Gitelson, M. (1952) 'The emotional position of the analyst in the psychoanalytic situation', *International Journal of Psycho-Analysis* 33: 1–10.

Glover, E. (1955) *The Technique of Psycho-Analysis*, New York: International Universities Press, 1968.

Greenberg, J.R. and Mitchell, S.A. (1983) *Object Relations in Psychoanalytic Theory*, Harvard University Press.

Greenson, R.R. (1967) *The Technique and Practice of Psycho-Analysis*, London: Hogarth Press.

Heimann, P. (1950) 'On counter-transference', *International Journal of Psycho-Analysis* 31: 81–4.

Hinshelwood, R.D. (1989) *A Dictionary of Kleinian Thought*, London: Free Association Books.

Hoffer, W. (1952) 'The mutual influences in the development of ego and id: earliest stages', *Psychoanalytic Study of the Child* 7: 31–41.

James, M. (1960) 'Premature ego development: some observations on disturbances in the first three months of life', *International Journal of Psycho-Analysis* 41: 288–94; also in G. Kohon (ed.) *The British School of Psychoanalysis: The Independent Tradition*, London: Free Association Books, 1986.

Jung, C.G. (1967) *Memories, Dreams, Reflections*, London: Collins.

Khan, M.M. (1974) *The Privacy of the Self*, London: Hogarth Press.

King, P. (1978) 'Affective response of the analyst to the patient's communications', *International Journal of Psycho-Analysis* 59: 329–34.

Klauber, J. *et al.* (1987) *Illusion and Spontaneity*, London: Free Association Books.

Klein, J. (1988) *Our Need for Others and its Roots in Infancy*, London: Tavistock.

Klein, M. (1932) 'The psycho-analysis of children', in *The Writings of Melanie Klein*, volume 2, London: Hogarth Press, 1975.
—— (1946) 'Notes on some schizoid mechanisms', in J. Riviere (ed.) *Developments in Psycho-Analysis*, London: Hogarth Press, 1952, pp. 292–320; also in *The Writings of Melanie Klein*, volume 3, *Envy and Gratitude and Other Works*, London: Hogarth Press, 1975, pp. 1–24.
—— (1961) 'Narrative of a Child Analysis', in *The Writings of Melanie Klein*, Volume 4, London: Hogarth Press, 1975.
Kohut, H. (1984) *How Does Analysis Cure?*, (ed.) A. Goldberg, Chicago: University of Chicago Press.
Laing, R.D. (1961) *The Self and Others*, London: Tavistock.
Langs, R.J. (1978) *The Listening Process*, New York: Aronson.
Laplanche, J. and Pontalis, J-B. (1973) *The Language of Psychoanalysis*, London: Hogarth Press.
Little, M. (1951) 'Counter-transference and the patient's response to it', *International Journal of Psycho-Analysis* 32: 32–40.
—— (1985) 'Winnicott working in areas where psychotic anxieties predominate: a personal record', *Free Associations* 3: 9–42.
—— (1987) 'On the value of regression to dependence', *Free Associations* 10: 7–22.
Matte Blanco, I. (1975) *The Unconscious as Infinite Sets*, London: Duckworth.
Mehler, J.A. and Argentieri, S. (1989) 'Hope and hopelessness: a technical problem?', *International Journal of Psycho-Analysis* 70: 295–304.
Milner, M. (1952) 'Aspects of symbolism in comprehension of the not-self', *International Journal of Psycho-Analysis* 33: 181–95.
Moberly, E.R. (1985) *The Psychology of Self and Other*, London: Tavistock.
Muir, E. (1960) *Collected Poems*, London: Faber, 1984.
Olinick, S.L. (1982) 'Meanings beyond words: psychoanalytic perceptions of silence and communication, happiness, sexual love and death', *International Review of Psychoanalysis* 9: 461–72.
O'Shaughnessy, E. (1983) 'Words and working through', *International Journal of Psycho-Analysis* 64: 281–9; also in *Melanie Klein Today*, Volume 2, London: Routledge, 1988.
Priestley, J.B. (1972) *Over the Long High Wall*, London: Heinemann.
Reich, A. (1951) 'On counter-transference', *International Journal of Psycho-Analysis* 32: 25–31.
Rosenfeld, H. (1987) *Impasse and Interpretation*, London: Tavistock.
Rycroft, C. (1968) *Imagination and Reality*, New York: International Universities Press.
—— (1972) *A Critical Dictionary of Psychoanalysis*, London: Penguin.
Samuels, A. (1985) *Jung and the Post-Jungians*, London: Routledge & Kegan Paul.
—— (1989) *The Plural Psyche*, London: Routledge.
Sandler, J.J. (1976) 'Countertransference and role-responsiveness', *International Review of Psycho-Analysis* 3: 43–7.

—— (1983) 'Reflections on some relations between psychoanalytic concepts and psychoanalytic practice', *International Journal of Psycho-Analysis* 64: 35–45.

Stewart, H. (1990) 'Interpretation and other agents for psychic change', *International Review of Psycho-Analysis*, 17: 61–70.

Strachey, J. (1934) 'The nature of the therapeutic interaction of psychoanalysis', *International Journal of Psycho-Analysis* 15: 127–59.

Symington, N. (1980) 'The response aroused by the psychopath', *International Review of Psycho-Analysis* 7: 291–8.

—— (1983) 'The analyst's act of freedom as agent of therapeutic change', *International Review of Psycho-Analysis* 10: 283–91.

Tansey, M.H. and Burke, W.F. (1985) 'Projective identification and the empathic process', *Contemporary Psychoanalysis* 21: 42–69.

Tuckett, D. (1983) 'Words and the psychoanalytic interaction', *International Review of Psycho-Analysis* 10: 407–13.

Winnicott, D.W. (1958) *Collected Papers: through Paediatrics to Psycho-Analysis*, London: Tavistock.

—— (1965) *Maturational Processes and the Facilitating Environment*, London: Hogarth Press.

—— (1971) *Playing and Reality*, London: Tavistock.

—— (1988) *Human Nature*, London: Free Association Books.

—— (1989) *Psycho-Analytic Explorations*, (eds) C. Winnicott, R. Shepherd, M. Davis, London: Karnac.

Name index

Alexander, F. 2, 10, 91–2, 102, 107
Argentieri, S. 182n

Balint, M. 132, 181n
Bateson, G. 178n
Beckett, S. 161
Bion, W.R. 1, 10, 111, 130
Blum, H.P. 181n
Bollas, C. 110, 179n, 184n
Boris, H.N. 182n
Bowlby, J. 181n
Burke, W.F. 179n

Daws, D. 178–9n

Eliot, T.S. 29–30

Fink, K. 179–80n
Freud, S.: and feeding patient 95; and free association 160; theories 168; on time and the unconscious 88, 180n; on words and things 181n

Gill, M.M. 76
Gitelson, M. 177n
Glover, E. 170
Greenberg, J.R. 184n
Greenson, R.R. 169

Heimann, P. 12
Hinshelwood, R.D. 177n
Hoffer, W. 75

James, M. 86
Jung, C.G. 180n

Khan, M.M. 75
King, P. 8, 129
Klauber, J. 75, 76, 179n
Klein, J. 181n, 184n
Klein, M. 32, 168, 169–70, 177n
Kohut, H. 168, 181n

Laing, R.D. 178n
Langs, R.J. 13, 21, 76, 83
Laplanche, J. 75, 76
Little, M. 12, 13, 97, 160, 180n

Matte Blanco, I. 76, 179n
Mehler, J.A. 182n
Milner, M. 158
Mitchell, S.A. 184n
Moberly, E.R. 91
Muir, E. 176

Olinick, S.L. 181n
O'Shaughnessy, E. 181n

Pontalis, J-B. 75, 76
Priestley, J.B. 14–15

Reich, A. 177n
Rosenfeld, H. 12–13, 183n
Rycroft, C. 181n

Samuels, A. 179n
Sandler, J.J. 8, 119, 129, 165, 184n

Subject index

abandonment 23–4, 85–6, 87–8, 102–4, 126–7, 149–50

absence: of analyst 78–9, 139; of anger 23–4; of feelings 8; of patient, from sessions 23–4; of sexuality 69–72

actualization 8, 129

ageing, and emotional scars 19–20

aggressor, identification with 8, 103, 128–30, 146–7

analysis: caricature of 20–2; ending of 181n, 182n; holiday breaks 21–2, 149; horizontal and vertical 76; lateness for 22, 119–20, 156; therapeutic benefit 90–2, 105–6; training in 107–9, 181n, 184n; traumatic effects 75, 82–6; *see also* process; space

analyst: able to tolerate patient's feelings 85–6, 88, 98, 104–5; absence of 78–9, 139; allowing time for transference 12; availability of 12, 95–6; bullying patient 160, 183n; character rationalized as technique 83, 168; 'destruction' of 98; detachment *vs.* involvement 165–7; environmental provision 2, 131–3, 135–6; failure of, patient's use of 11, 120–1; independent 14; insecurity of 19, 31; need for flexibility 65–6, 83–6, 89, 167–9; patient's need to use 97–8; perceived as critical 140; perceived as defensive 140–1; perceived as intrusive 141–2; reorientation by patient 20; style of interpretation 131–2; *see also* technique

anger: analyst perceived as able to tolerate 85–6, 88; and cancelled session 139; expressed by silence and absence 23–4; and similarity in transference 80–1

anthropology 4

'antisocial tendency' 115–16

anxiety, signal 76–9

assumptions 153–4; *see also* preconceptions

availability: of analyst 12, 95–6; of mother 93

bad object, analyst used to represent 11, 87

balance: control 94; similarity and difference 79–82, 88–9

behaviour: 'antisocial' 115–16; as communication 22–4, 123–4, 143; sadistic 123

'better parent' *see under* parent

boredom, analyst's 67–8

boundaries 118, 159, 160; *see also* space, analytic

breaks, in therapy 21–2, 149

breastfeeding 95–6, 111–12

British Psycho-Analytical Society 14, 177n

bullying, by analyst 160, 183n

caricature, of analysis 20–2

castration anxiety 17–18
catatonia 9
certainty, dogmatic 5–6, 15;
    resisting 13–14
character, analyst's 83, 168
children: 'antisocial tendency'
    115–16; developmental needs
    93–4, 113–15, 160, 183–4n
cliché interpretation 17–30; by
    patient 26–9; mistaken
    responses to patient's
    communication 19–26
communication: behaviour as
    22–4, 123–4, 143; and
    countertransference 8; difficulty
    in 25–6, 83; mistaken 19–26;
    through play 31–64 *passim*;
    projective identification as 8;
    unconscious 110
conflict, unconscious 2
confrontation 142–3
consistency, need for 97, 114
contrast, pain of 106–7, 166–7
control: of analytic process 164–5;
    need for 58, 183n
corrective emotional experience 2,
    10–11, 87–8, 90–2, 102
countertransference 7, 12; and
    communication 8; diagnostic
    165; different uses of 142–3;
    hate in 67; and interpretation
    65–74, 179n; personal 8, 67
creativity 161–3
cues, from patient 33, 64–6, 105–6;
    allowing for 83; *see also* hope

defecation 67, 69, 173–5
delinquency 115
demands, libidinal 90, 111; *see also*
    needs
depression, post-natal 102, 178–9n
despair 121–2
development, child: and hope
    113–15; needs 113–15, 160, 183n
diagnostic countertransference 165
diagnostic response 8, 165
dilemma, dealing with 156
discovery, *vs.* imposition/provision

2, 6, 29–30, 73–4, 90–2, 105–6,
    109, 169
dogma 5–6, 13
double-bind 25–6, 178n

ego-needs 90
ending, of analysis 124, 181n, 182n
enuresis 117
environmental failure 11, 86,
    126–7
environmental provision by analyst
    2, 131–3, 135–6
examples: ageing and emotional
    scars 19–20; analyst perceived as
    critical 140; analyst perceived as
    defensive 140–1; analyst
    perceived as intrusive 141–2;
    analyst's involvement in analytic
    process 166–7; analytic holding
    87–8, 89, 181n; anger, expressed
    by silence and absence 23–4;
    'better parent', failure 99–102,
    104; castration anxiety 17–18;
    child's unconscious search for
    help 31–64; cliché-thinking by
    patient 26–9; communication
    difficulty 25–6; contrast 102–5;
    countertransference and
    interpretation 65–74; different
    kinds of play 162–3; different
    uses of the countertransference
    142–3; environmental failure
    126–7; inner world realized
    127–31; length of interpretation
    144; need for firmness 114–15;
    pain of contrast 106–7;
    pre-delinquent behaviour 116;
    profound experience 172–5; re-
    enactment 133–5; regression
    assumed 20–2;
    role-responsiveness and unmet
    need 119–20; silent trauma 84–6;
    similarity and transference 80–1;
    unconscious sets 76–9

failure: to adapt, progressive 86;
    analyst's, patient's use of 11, 86,
    120–1; 'better parent' 11, 81,